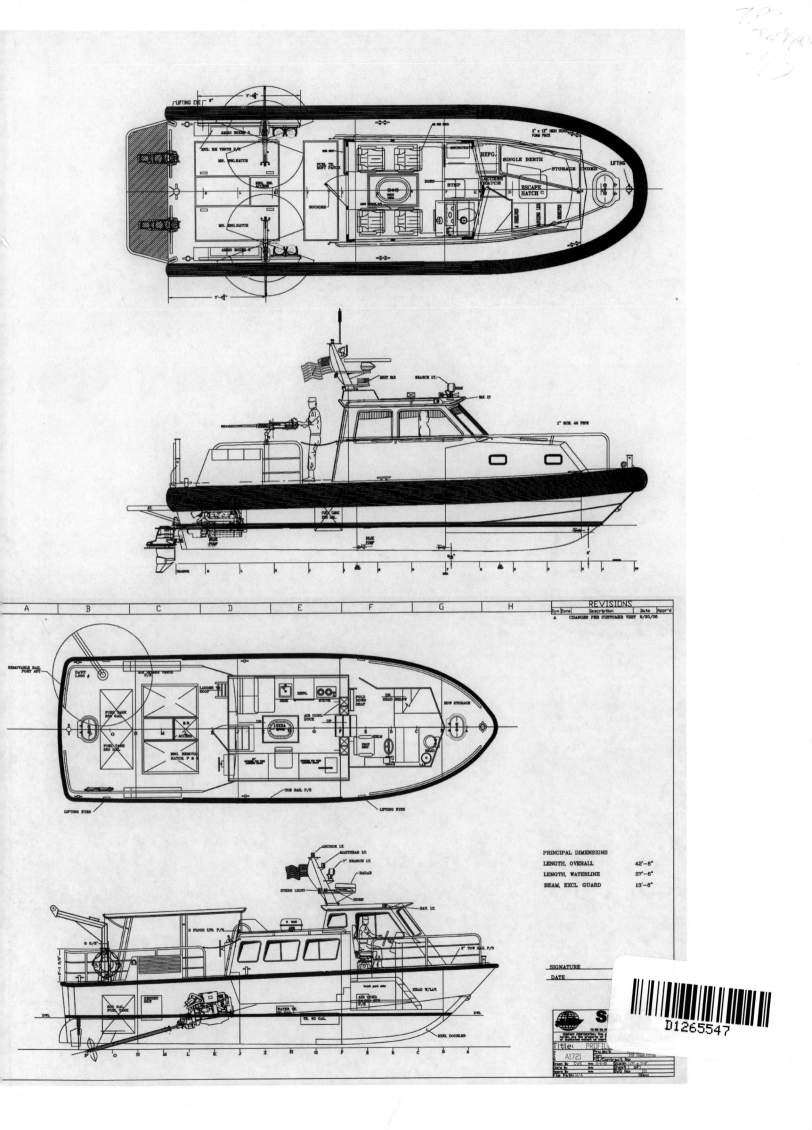

D1265547

HARD WORK, GOOD PEOPLE,
and
100,000 BOATS

5O

**YEARS OF
BOAT-BUILDING
WITH
ZACH McCLENDON, JR.**

THE
DONNING COMPANY
PUBLISHERS

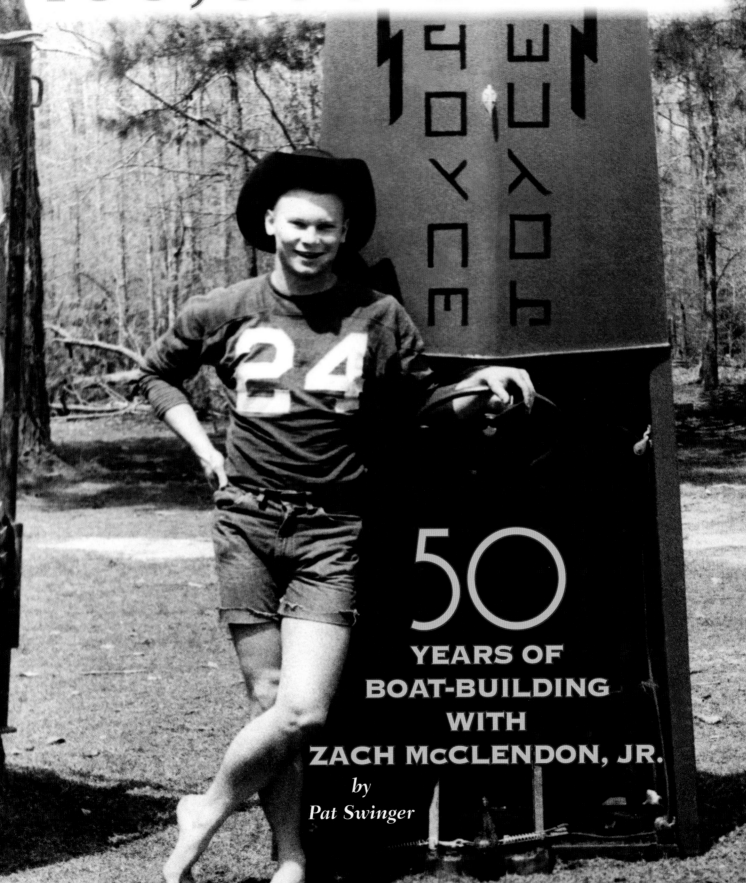

HARD WORK, GOOD PEOPLE,
and
100,000 BOATS

50 YEARS OF BOAT-BUILDING WITH ZACH McCLENDON, JR.

by

Pat Swinger

ACKNOWLEDGMENTS

Assembling all the details of a company's history is seldom as easy as one might think and I would like to express my appreciation for the dedication and perseverance that John and Robin McClendon displayed in the assembling of this book. I would like to thank them for the countless hours they spent recalling and relating the many stories and images that make up the life of their father, Zach McClendon, Jr., and the companies to which he has dedicated himself for the past fifty years.

I would also like to thank the people who gave of their time to relate the stories of MonArk's early days: Ron Echols, Larry Flemister, Bobby Jack Flemister, Dick Dickinson, Elmo Judkins, and Johnny Smith. Their help was invaluable. It has been an honor to be a small part of the MonArk/SeaArk family.

Pat Swinger

Copyright © 2009 by SeaArk Marine and Pat Swinger

All rights reserved, including the right to reproduce this work in any form whatsoever without permission in writing from the publisher, except for brief passages in connection with a review. For information, please write:

The Donning Company Publishers
184 Business Park Drive, Suite 206
Virginia Beach, VA 23462

Steve Mull, General Manager
Barbara Buchanan, Office Manager
Heather L. Floyd, Editor
Lori Wiley, Graphic Designer
Derek Eley, Imaging Artist
Cindy Smith, Project Research Coordinator
Tonya Hannink, Marketing Specialist
Pamela Engelhard, Marketing Advisor

Neil Hendricks, Project Director

Cataloging-in-Publication Data

Swinger, Patricia, 1951-
    Hard work, good people, and 100,000 boats : 50 years of boat-building with Zach McClendon / by Pat Swinger.
       p. cm.
    Includes bibliographical references.
    ISBN 978-1-57864-576-3 (hardcover : alk. paper)
    1. Boatbuilding--Arkansas--History. 2. MonArk Boat Company--History. 3. SeaArk Boats--History. 4.
McClendon, Zach. 5. McClendon, Zach--Family. 6. Boatbuilders--Arkansas--Biography. 7. Monticello (Ark.)--
Biography. I. Title. II. Title: Hard work, good people, and one hundred thousand boats. III. Title: Hard work, good
people, and a hundred thousand boats.
    VM321.52.U6S94 2009
    338.7'6238230922--dc22
                                    2009021284

Printed in the United States of America at Walsworth Publishing Company

TABLE OF CONTENTS

U.S. HOUSE OF REPRESENTATIVES

June 11, 2008

MIKE ROSS
FOURTH DISTRICT
ARKANSAS

Mr. Zach McClendon
PO Box 210
Monticello, AR 71655

Dear Mr. McClendon:

I would like to congratulate you on your well-deserved 50th Anniversary of doing business in Arkansas! This is a tremendous accomplishment and you should be very proud of this milestone.

I admire all the hard work and dedication you have provided to successfully remain a world leader in boat design and manufacturing. SeaArk's products operate in all 50 states and in over 50 different countries, and your uncompromising quality sets the standard of excellence in the boating industry.

From your start with flat bottom aluminum Jon boats in 1959, to your now more riveted and specialized boats, you have shown a tremendous perseverance to withstand and succeed in the test of time. You have also always embodied a company who takes pride in their team and values a close relationship with its over 250 employees. Therefore, your 50th Anniversary Celebration merits great respect and admiration for you and your family. I look forward to your continued service in providing quality boats to the world, and I am proud of the many contributions you make to our great state as a true Arkansas company!

Again, congratulations on this esteemed landmark and I wish you the very best in all the years to come.

Sincerely,

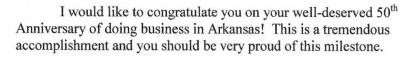

Mike Ross

314 CANNON BUILDING, WASHINGTON, D.C. 20515

MARK PRYOR
ARKANSAS

United States Senate

August 6, 2008

Mr. Zach McClendon
Post Office Box 210
Monticello, Arkansas 71657

Dear Mr. McClendon:

I want to congratulate you as you celebrate 50 years in business at SeaArk
Marine/SeaArk Boats. This is a great accomplishment and I know you and
your family must be proud.

Our state is a better place because of the hard work and dedication that you
have provided. I join with others in thanking you for your contributions to
the community.

Happy 50th anniversary to you and the SeaArk team. Wishing you the very
best for future endeavors.

Sincerely,

Mark Pryor

STATE OF ARKANSAS
MIKE BEEBE
GOVERNOR

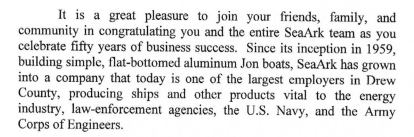

Mr. Zach McClendon
SeaArk Marine, Inc.
Post Office Box 210
Monticello, AR 71655

Dear Zach:

It is a great pleasure to join your friends, family, and community in congratulating you and the entire SeaArk team as you celebrate fifty years of business success. Since its inception in 1959, building simple, flat-bottomed aluminum Jon boats, SeaArk has grown into a company that today is one of the largest employers in Drew County, producing ships and other products vital to the energy industry, law-enforcement agencies, the U.S. Navy, and the Army Corps of Engineers.

In an increasingly competitive and complex marketplace, you have proven your ability to serve the needs of the public and to earn the trust of those who put their confidence in you. You have built SeaArk's success and its reputation by providing high-quality products for private recreation and for the public good. Your selection reflects your widespread influence, as well as the positive effect you have had on others through your work and through your actions. On behalf of the State of Arkansas, best wishes for continued success.

Sincerely,

Mike Beebe

MB:jb

September 2009

DEDICATION

While fifty years of continuous ownership and operation is a noble achievement for any family business, it is almost unheard of in the marine industry. This book and the story it relates is dedicated to our father, Zach McClendon, Jr., and all the people who were, are, and will be along on this amazing journey that he started back in May of 1958.

It cannot be overstated that working alongside one's family members is uniquely challenging in many ways. The desire to please goes well beyond that of normal professional achievement. When one's father is also their boss, the family dynamics at work take on entirely new dimensions, not all of them positive. For anything that we might have lost in a moment of frustration over the years, we have gained much more from our dad and the wonderful team of people surrounding us as our extended family.

Zach McClendon, Jr. is an incredible man with an amazing story. As our father, he has protected and provided for us; as our mentor, he has taught us what we need to know most about life and business; as our leader, he has guided us through an increasingly com-plex and difficult industry; and as our friend, we have laughed together about it all along the way.

This book is a mere glimpse into a special man and his creations, triumphs, failures, challenges, and dreams. It would have taken a dozen volumes to tell every story that surfaced, so it was not possible to include them all. We wish to thank everyone who contributed—whether directly or unknowingly—to this work and the story that it tells.

Dad, we dedicate this work to you and all those wonderful people who shared your vision: some only for a moment, some for most of the last fifty years. What you have given us all is an opportunity to become something much more than we could have been without you.

We could not have asked for a better man to be our father or a better group of people to turn dreams into reality.

With Love and Thanks,

Robin McClendon   John McClendon

Zach, Sr., Pauline, Zach, Jr., and Paddy.

Chapter One

THE McCLENDON CLAN

When the first of this McClendon clan left northern Scotland at the end of the seventeenth century, they settled in Perquimans County in the North Carolina colony.

The unforgiving terrain of the Scottish Highlands and centuries of clan warfare immutably molded the people of Scotland. Known for their stubbornness, industry, and frugality, traits that were necessary for survival and deeply ingrained, the Scots were no doubt equal to the challenges they faced as they carved out a place for themselves in the New World.

Many of the McClendons are listed in the rolls of the Revolutionary War and, as was common, some received land in return for their service. Over the next hundred years, they migrated south to Georgia and west into Mississippi, Alabama, Louisiana, and Texas. Some of the McClendons are recorded in Arkansas by the early decades of the nineteenth century. The family history mentions a headstone labeled "McClendon" found in Mount Zion Cemetery in Calhoun, Louisiana, giving testimony to the character that runs deep through the entire clan. It reads,

"A people sturdy as the oak,
Stalwart as the pine,
Gentle as the brook,
And enduring as the hills."

Zach McClendon, Sr.

So it was that Zach McClendon, Sr., along with two sisters and four brothers, grew up in Strong, Arkansas, in the Ouachita Bottoms. His father, known as Papa Sank by his grandchildren, first owned a sawmill and then, after moving to Strong, owned a cotton gin and a gristmill for grinding corn. Times were hard and the McClendons, like most families in that area, were "dirt floor poor" and yet, somehow, Zach, Sr. managed to attend two years of college in the late 1920s. As the Great Depression hit, he went to work for the Murray Company out of Dallas, selling cotton implement equipment and eventually began building the cotton gins himself. Naturally mechanically inclined, he'd honed his engineering and mechanical skills working with his father. Zach, Sr. was a cautious, calculating businessman who, in keeping with the times, never discarded anything. Through hard work and industry, he eventually owned a number of gins himself throughout the area, many built with little more than scrap metal.

Zach McClendon, Sr. and Pauline Johnson were married in March of 1933 in Strong, Arkansas. Their daughter, Paddy, was born the following December and Zach, Jr. came along in 1937. Zach, Sr. was selling equipment to the numerous cotton gins that dotted the South in the years just prior to World War II and when the war created a labor shortage, his employer offered him a job managing the Drew Cottonseed Oil Mill. The family moved to Monticello, Arkansas, in 1943, and when the war ended, Zach, Sr. began buying equity in the mill in addition to owning many of the cotton gins that supplied the oil mill.

Like many men of his time working hard to provide for his family through the Great Depression, Zach, Sr. was shaped by these lean years. Zach, Jr. recalls that his father, like most men of his day, didn't have a lot of time for play with his family and had no time for hobbies, spending all his time on the hard work it took

Zach, Jr. as a toddler on a traditional cotton wagon, circa 1938.

Zach, Sr. and Zach, Jr. take to the water in the 1940s. Zach, Jr. displayed an enjoyment of water-related recreation and sports throughout his life.

The house in Monticello where Zach, Sr. and Pauline raised daughter Paddy and son Zach, Jr. The McClendons came to Monticello in the 1940s after living in the small town of Strong, Arkansas.

to provide for them. John McClendon remembers his grandfather, who was naturally quiet and reserved, as being "kind, but dead serious," and Robin remembers him telling her she was getting "a bag of switches for Christmas," secure in the knowledge that he was only teasing his "Gal Baby."

Later in their life together, Zach, Sr. and Pauline were able to enjoy some travels and John recalls his grandmother saying that Zach, Sr. would strike up a conversation with anybody and everybody and loved learning about anything new. Given another time and a different set of circumstances, Zach, Sr. was the kind of man who would likely have seized the opportunity to further his education.

Zach McClendon, Jr.

Zach, Jr., known as Sonny, grew up like any other boy in a small town, exploring the woods and creeks near Monticello. His love and deep appreciation for nature comes from the time he spent on the Saline River

Legendary Frugality

Frugality is a hallmark trait among Scots and the McClendons are no exception. Unable to afford new equipment, Zach recalls that his father was always building things "the poor boy way," scouring his pile of scrap metal for bits and pieces. Zach's mother, Pauline, was likewise frugal, following the homemaker's creed to squeeze something out of every nickel earned by her husband's hard work. Despite his obvious success, Zach is still a frugal man and doesn't like to waste anything. He buys his reading glasses at Sam's, opting for the bargain five-pack for twenty dollars, and when he shows a visitor through his shed, he will point out a stack of emerald green scotch bottles that he intends, in his spare time, to turn into a chandelier for the lake house.

The legendary frugality of Zach, Sr. was at its best during the construction of a plant for Drew Foam, a company that he would start up in 1965. A new plant was built in the mid-1970s to accommodate the growing business. The maintenance chief, a man named Mr. Cooty, was in charge of supervising the construction. He went to Zach, Sr. with a list of electrical wire that he needed to wire the plant for electricity. Zach, Sr. looked at the list and advised Mr. Cooty that there was a pile of wire that had been saved and stored at the cottonseed oil mill. Mr. Cooty protested, telling Mr. McClendon that all of that wire was in pieces that were only three feet long or less. Zach, Sr. looked at him in all seriousness and asked, "Ain't you got no tape?"

Known as somewhat of a scrounger himself, Zach, Jr. once purchased a second-hand Niagara hydraulic break press for next to nothing from an abandoned factory. Then, in 1994, instead of paying $700,000 for a brand-new plasma cutter, he put one together for $50,000, building the twenty-by-forty-foot table himself. His father would be proud.

hunting, fishing, and swimming with friends, though his first boat-building experience was on a pond near the family's original home on South Main Street. "It was a fifty-five-gallon oil drum with two old cross ties," he recalled. "I took barbed wire and latched them together. I had a cross tie on either side of the barrel. So you straddled the barrel, and then I cut a sapling to push the boat around the pond. I was probably eight years old when I did that. I loved water. I always have."

Later, the Boy Scouts provided an outlet for the energetic young Zach. Ron Echols, a childhood friend who later went to work with Zach at MonArk, knew Zach from their days in the Boy Scouts and recalled a trip they made to the Okefenokee Swamp in Georgia. Camping out in the swamp provided quite a few challenges, not the least of which was protecting their food supply from raccoons and other thieves. Luckily, Zach had built a chuck wagon chest he'd found in a Boy Scout magazine to protect their food. The trip must have been quite a thrill for a bunch of young boys from Monticello, but what stands out in Ron's memory the most is taking a boat out into the swamp and watching wide-eyed as Zach bailed into the water to wrestle a four-foot-long alligator. As Ron said, "Zach was very daring, and I'll just leave it at that."

Dick Dickinson, another childhood friend who later joined the MonArk team, also recalls that Zach exhibited some persuasive leadership abilities as a youngster. "Even when we were kids, Zach would always be the leader of the group," he said, and recalled a time in ninth grade when he, Zach, and another friend named Jerry Nichols came upon a creek while they were wandering through the woods in the dead of winter. The creek was frozen but Zach could see fish swimming below the thin layer of ice. Figuring the fish would be sluggish due to the cold, Zach convinced the boys to strip down to their skivvies to go fishing. Dick said, "Jerry ended up with a terrible cold, I ended up with pneumonia, but it didn't bother Zach a bit even though he was the first one in the water."

Zach became an Eagle Scout at the age of sixteen though sports, including his beloved hunting and fishing, dominated his high school years. Again demonstrating his leadership qualities, Zach became the captain of Monticello High School's football team. Zach's football claim to fame occurred in a game between Monticello High and Crossett High in which he blocked Barry Switzer, who went on to become an All American at the University of Arkansas and later national championship-winning coach at the University of Oklahoma. But nothing shaped young Zach McClendon, nor foreshadowed his future, more than the organization he and three of his friends formed.

Shack & Company

It all started when Zach was about thirteen years old. He and three friends, Ronnie James, Bob McGarr, and Jerry Nichols, spent time fishing and swimming together and liked to camp on Indian Soap Creek. Needing a place to store their fishing gear, they commandeered an old tin

Zach experimented with boat-building even as a young boy.

Zach McClendon, Sr., early 1940s.

Zach, Jr. in full ceremonial Indian dance team dress for a Boy Scout Order of the Arrow ceremony, circa 1952.

PHONE 59

ZACH McCLENDON, PRESIDENT

Drew Cotton Seed Oil Mill

Manufacturers of

Cottonseed Products, Ice, & Concrete Products

P. O. BOX 210
MONTICELLO, ARKANSAS

Drew Cotton Seed Oil Mill letterhead. SeaArk Marine still has the same post office box number.

Value

From time to time, Zach admittedly allowed himself to be swayed by MonArk's salesmen, who encouraged him to change a boat design or more often to find a way to lower the price of a product. But Zach had learned from his father how important it was to respect and value your product. After all, if you don't, how can you expect someone else to value it?

When they first started building boats, Zach, Sr. was still involved in the business. However, the cottonseed mill was still the main business and the boats were considered a side business. One day, a guy came by wanting to purchase a couple of boats. The guy told Zach, Sr., "I'll buy a couple of boats, but I want you to throw in a bag of that cottonseed meal." Zach, Sr. refused. He wouldn't "throw in" a dollar's worth of cottonseed meal in order to sell the boats. "You're either gonna buy the boat or you're not gonna buy the boat," he said. The moral of the story—there's no such thing as a free bag of cottonseed meal.

Zach and Joyce, the first powered boat he constructed, on land and in the water.

The Shack Queen, *built on oil drums, was kept at Longview on the Saline River. According to Zach, "We loved that boat. Man, we thought we had a ChrisCraft."*

shack in the McClendons' back yard, put a floor in it, and turned it into their headquarters, giving birth to Shack & Company. This, however, was no ordinary boys' club.

Each of the boys held an office with clearly defined responsibilities. They organized float trips down the Saline River and took a memorable trip to Paradise Lake on the Mississippi River. The boys shared experiences in the Boy Scouts, played football together in high school, and hunted and fished whenever possible. Together, they built their first powered boat, named *Joyce* after Zach's girlfriend, and christened it with a one-dollar bottle of wine. It was a small 8-foot boat, but the fun they had building it inspired them to tackle building a houseboat. Named the *Shack Queen*, it boasted hot and cold running water, a hi-fi record player (reflecting the audio equipment of the day), a radio, a butane heater, a Mississippi riverboat-style gangplank, a sundeck, and a kitchen, complete with an oven and icebox. Two outboard motors gave the *Shack Queen* a cruising speed of about seven miles an hour.

Every event or project Shack & Company undertook originated with a budget based on what the boys could pitch in and was strictly adhered to. Their biggest project, one that made headlines in the *Arkansas Democrat*, was the dance they held in July 1957. By now, their membership had swelled to eight, and most of them were attending college. They set out to throw the biggest party in Monticello's history—and they succeeded.

The only place in town big enough to hold a dance of this magnitude was at the Drew Cottonseed Oil Mill, a 60-by-180-foot storage house. To use it, however, they would have to move 211 tons of dusty cottonseed. Working seventeen hours a day for seven days living on lemonade, popcorn, and cheese dip supplied by their girlfriends, they finally managed to move the mountain of seeds to a building across the street. Using borrowed fire hoses to wash out the remaining dust, they then decorated the warehouse with 1,920 feet of aluminum foil and 22,000 feet of blue and white crepe paper lit with changing colored lights.

Formal invitations were printed and sent to young people throughout the Delta and as far away as New York and Alaska. And lest anyone think they'd not set their sights high enough, one invitation even went to President and Mrs. Eisenhower. When the night of the party arrived, 400 people showed up to dance to the sounds of The Czars of Rhythm.

As the boys grew into young men, the organization itself changed from a self-proclaimed "good-time group" to one in which the members encouraged each other to at least ponder their futures. They talked about forming an investor's club to buy up land in the Delta they loved in order to protect it. Filled with the audacity of youth, they had dreams of seeing the state of Arkansas develop Texan-sized pride. When interviewed for the July 7, 1957 issue of the *Arkansas Democrat*, Zach said, "A Shack man has to be a gentleman and a scholar—and a sportsman." The reporter noted a pause before Zach continued saying, "Everything's proved out except the scholarship business. Some of us did good to get through high school."

It wouldn't be surprising to find that many of the members of Shack & Company went on to become successful entrepreneurs. What is surprising, though, is that in the same article, Shack & Company's presi-

Bait-A-Spot

Zach's first entrepreneurial inspiration came to him when he was no more than ten years old. His father had taken a job with the Drew Cottonseed Oil Mill and moved the family to Monticello. After the cotton was ginned, the seed was sent to the oil mill where the cotton residue was removed, and then the seed was crushed into a pulp and cooked to remove the oil. What remained after that process was a hard cake, which was ground up into cottonseed meal, mixed with the hulls that came off the seed, and used for cattle feed. Since cottonseed meal is high in protein, it makes a very effective natural fertilizer and is still used for cattle feed to this day.

Zach's idea was to take that cake of cottonseed meal, cut it into chunks, and tie it up into a cloth bag. His plan was to call it "Bait-A-Spot" and sell it to fishermen who were patient enough to drop the bag filled with cottonseed meal into the water and wait for it to attract the hungry and unwitting fish below.

Alas, the complexities of marketing and distribution dashed the young boy's dream. As Zach recalls, "Back then we didn't have the big sport warehouse stores so we didn't have any way to market it." When relating this story, Zach admitted that he hadn't thought of "Bait-A-Spot" for a long time. Decades later, and with a laundry list of businesses and products under his belt, Zach just might be ready to give this one another shot.

Moving the 211 tons of cottonseed was a tough and dusty job.

Shack & Company. Front: Benny Roark, Zach McClendon, Jr., Jerry Lynn Nichols, Ronnie James, and Ronnie Echols. Back: Buddy Griffith and Freddy Smith. Bob McGarr was in Maryland for the summer.

dent, Zach McClendon, who the author described as a "born executive," listed the current members and their offices, and described one of the other members as "the dreamer of the bunch." Whatever the other members of Shack and Company ultimately went on to achieve, it's hard to imagine anyone being more of a dreamer than Zach McClendon himself.

Like his father, Zach, Jr. loves learning and never misses an opportunity—on a plane, at a boat show or trade show, or even at a restaurant—to meet someone and strike up a conversation. It doesn't really matter what the topic of conversation might be because as he so often says, "You might learn something."

Sources:

"A History of the McClendon Family in America," compiled by
    J. Connor McClendon.
Arkansas Democrat, Sunday issue, July 7, 1957.

Shack & Company in front of the McClendon home, circa 1956.

SHACK & Co. Has a Ball

Some ex-Boy Scouts have put away their merit badges and become the hosts with the most in Monticello.

DON'T BE TOO SURPRISED IF YOU read in the papers a few years from now that the entire Delta area of southeast Arkansas has been bought by a corporation called Shack & Company.

Shack & Company is a unique organization of eight young men that has never failed in anything it has undertaken. And it has tried a lot of things—from building a luxury house-boat to throwing the biggest party ever seen in Monticello, which is Shack's home base.

The party was a dance that Shack gave last month. It turned out to be proof positive that Shack could do anything it set out to do. For one thing, the only place big enough for the dance was the Drew Cotton Seed Oil Mill, a 60 by 180-foot cotton seed storage house. Using it gave them almost 11,000 square feet of floor space to play with, but it involved the moving of 211 tons of cotton seed.

Shack members shoveled loose cotton seed until they couldn't breathe—"because the dust from the seed was so thick." But they worked 17 hours a day for seven days and took just enough time out to consume the lemonade, pop-corn and cheese dip that girl friends brought in.

WHEN ALL THE SEEDS WERE MOVED to a building across the street, they borrowed fire hoses to wash out the huge building. It took about an hour to get the water inside the building, and more than two days to get it all out. Then they decorated the place with 1,920 feet of aluminum foil and 22,000 feet of blue and white crepe paper and equipped it with changing, colored lights.

Townspeople were dropping by to see the converted seed mill for a solid week before the dance. Monticello is a college town, but it had never seen anyone go to so much trouble for a party.

The list of invited guests included President and Mrs. Eisenhower, Governor and Mrs. Faubus and "everyone else we could think of." That included every young person—from high school juniors to college seniors—in the Delta. And to Shack, the Delta means "from Dumas to the Louisiana line and from Monticello to the Mississippi river." The printed invitations went to Mississippi, Tennessee, Texas, Oklahoma, Missouri, New York, the Carolinas, Alaska and Washington, D. C. When the big

night of June 8 rolled around, more than 400 guests showed up; it was quite a party.

But it was just another page in Shack's colorful seven-year history, which started with four youngsters in Monticello who liked to camp overnight on Indian Soap creek. Their interests were the same, and so they stuck together. Today, there are seven members—and a lot more boys who'd like to be.

SHACK'S ... don jr., is a ...

outdoorsman; before college, most of his life was spent in the woods and on the water. But because he thinks like an executive and has a driving forcefulness to back it up, Shack & Company has held together a n d prospered through the years.

Every member holds an office, and in

Over 400 people showed up to dance to The Czars of Rhythm at Monticello's biggest party ever in July 1957. Photo courtesy of the Arkansas Democrat-Gazette, Inc.

Displaying their gentlemanly ways, Shack & Company even had formal invitations printed.

SHACK AND COMPANY

INVITES YOU AND A DATE
TO A DANCE

**ON SATURDAY, JUNE 8TH, 1957
FROM 9 P. M. TO 1 A. M.**

AT DREW COTTON SEED OIL MILL
MONTICELLO, ARKANSAS
SEMI-FORMAL

MUSIC PROVIDED BY
"THE CZARS OF RHYTHM"

ZACH McCLENDON	BUDDY GRIFFITH	JERRY NICHOLS	RONNIE JAMES
FREDDY SMITH	BOBBY McGARR	RONNIE ECHOLS	BENNY ROARK

MonArk catalog, 1960s.

Chapter Two

THE BIRTH OF MONARK BOATS

Most people who know Zach McClendon would have guessed that a future in boats was all but inevitable for the young man, but if you ask him what he thought his future held, he will tell you, "As a kid, I thought I was going to be a scientist. I've always loved nature… animals, plants, and bugs."

Even though his father's business did very well in Monticello, Zach confesses that he always had it in the back of his mind that it simply wouldn't be possible to make the kind of money he wanted to make in little Monticello, Arkansas. "You can make something there," he explained, "but if you're limited to selling it there, you're not going to make a lot of money."

The night of his graduation from Monticello High School, Zach and some other friends, Freddy Smith and Bud Bulloch among them, headed for Alaska. Over the summer, they each cleared $900 working on the railroad. Zach's mother wanted him to go to Davidson College, a Presbyterian school in North Carolina. He complied with her wishes that fall, but soon found that he was unsuited for the East Coast culture. Away from the lakes, rivers, and woods of Arkansas, Zach was the proverbial fish out of water. The following year, he re-turned to his home state and attended the University of Arkansas at Fayetteville.

Ask Zach McClendon what *really* led him to the boat business and, at a loss for words, he agrees that it was probably providence, adding, "My whole life has been like that." If that's the case, then providence came in the form of Norris O. Judkins and Zach, Sr. while Zach was still at the University of Arkansas. "My dad called me one day (he knew I liked boats) and said, 'This guy, Norris Judkins, had worked at DuraCraft and has a one-man shop building awnings. He's built himself a jon boat, built one for a friend, and we might put something together with him,'" Zach recalled. "I said, 'Yes sir. When do you want me to come home?'"

The Ward brothers, Bill and Chick, were the first to begin the boat-building business in Monticello. During World War II, they made aluminum parts for the military in their blacksmith machine shop. Looking for something to do with the remaining aluminum once the war was over, they built an aluminum craft patterned on the flat bottom boats built from cypress wood that were commonly used throughout the region. Being avid hunters and fishermen like most folks in the area, building boats was a natural fit. "They hit it just right after the war," Zach commented. "People had money to buy stuff with. Their business took off, and they became one of the biggest aluminum boat builders in the country as Dura-Craft Boat Company."

Norris contributed his equipment to the deal—a hand break press, unishears, one or two welders, and a couple of spray paint guns—all told about $2,000 worth of equipment. Zach, Sr. put up $2,000 for himself and $2,000 for his son. The McClendons agreed to be fifty/fifty partners with Norris when they started up.

That was in 1958 and only a few companies were building aluminum boats: Alumacraft of Minnesota, Lone Star in Texas, and Grumman in New York among them.

A pick-up truck similar to this one was used to carry MonArk jon boats in the early years. Zach, Jr. was told not to come home until he had sold the entire truckload.

Elmo Judkins, son of N. O. Judkins, 2008. Elmo was one of MonArk's first hires and recalled that he was "the one that cut out the first MonArk boat."

One of the McClendons' earliest employees, Royce Doggett, came up with the MonArk name in tribute to Monticello, Arkansas. The little company began building ten boats at a time—12-foot riveted aluminum jon boats—setting up a welding shop in the cottonseed house on Conley Street in Monticello. Once built, they were loaded into the back of Norris Judkins's 1949 Chevy pick-up with a steel rack on the back. Zach took off down the road, peddling the boats to gas stations, mom-and-pop grocery stores, bait shops, and anyone else who would buy them. The MonArk name wasn't yet known, but despite the discouragement that inevitably follows rejection, Zach wouldn't go home until the entire truckload of boats was sold.

They went on to build 14-foot boats, then a wider 14-footer, and eventually a 16-foot boat. Norris hired his son, Elmo Judkins, and most of the manufacturing tools they needed for their expanding product line came from the homegrown talent of Zach, Sr. and Elmo. "My dad never believed in buying anything new," Zach said, adding, "We didn't have any money and he was a great homemade engineer. He always had a pile of scrap iron and if we said we needed to build something, he'd say, 'Well, let's see what we've got out here.' He and Elmo made a rib press out of an old cottonseed press and some cottonseed plates made of three-fourths-inch steel," Zach recalled. "Elmo was a very talented machinist—he could do anything."

MonArk ALL ALUMINUM BOATS
Built By A Fisherman For A Fisherman

The MonArk Fisherman is a fisherman's dream. Designed so that it is easy to maneuver in those hard-to-get-to-places. The boat that is simply styled stressing safety and satisfaction. The all aluminum MonArk is rigidly constructed and so durable that it should last a lifetime. It has comfortable seats packed with STYRO-FOAM to make it the safest fishing boat afloat. Its lightness in weight makes it the perfect car-top boat.

Seamless pressed ribs are designed for maximum strength and are closed at the top for safety and convenience in keeping boats clean.

All aluminum construction offers maintenance free service.

Heavy extruded caprail gives the MonArk that extra stiffness it needs for rough water and large motors. The lip-over makes the boat extremely easy to load and unload.

MonArk boats feature heavy duty bow and transom handles, two fish-stringer loops at each seat, heavy duty transom braces, runners, and sprayrails.

Standard equipment includes drainplugs and seat brackets. Hulls are formed from a single piece of tough full temper aluminum alloy. Arched ribs provide drainage from bow to stern. Built in styro-foam flotation insures against sinking, even with full load.

Standard colors are Marine Gray or natural finish.

Olive-drab coloring for duck hunters and live-bait wells optional.

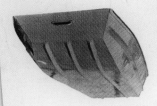

SPECIFICATIONS

Model No.	958	1251	1258	1451	1458	1464	1664
Length	9'	12'	12'	14'	14'	14'	14'
Transom Width	44"	40"	44"	40"	44"	49"	49"
Beam Width	48"	45"	48"	45"	48"	56"	54"
Bottom Width	32"	30"	32"	30"	32"	34"	34"
Bow Width	36"	32"	34"	32"	34"	42"	42"
Transom Height	15"	15"	15"	15"	15"	15"	15"
Side Depth	15"	14"	15"	14"	15"	18"	18"
Rec. H.P.	3	5	5	7½	7½	15	15
Rec. Passengers	2	2	2	3	3	4	4
Gauge Hull	.058	.051	.058	.051	.058	.064	.064
Gauge Transom	.064	.064	.064	.064	.064	.064	.064
Approx. Wt.	75 lb.	95 lb.	105 lb.	115 lb.	140 lb.	165 lb.	190 lb.
Color	Marine Gray or natural finish, Olive Drab for duck hunters, optional.						

Specifications and Prices Subject to Change Without Notice

MonArk's first promotional brochure, 1960.

The back cover of MonArk's 1965 catalog shows a young Robin and her mother, Dianne (second from right), enjoying the pontoon.

MonArk Model P1028

MonArk

MONTICELLO, ARKANSAS 71655
501 EM 7-5363 • 501 EM 7-3348

Also manufacturer of a complete line of recreational vehicles, houseboats, jumbo ice chests, tool chests and other related marine aluminum products.

Betty Brinkley and Barbara Rush, both from Arkansas, sit in a MonArk canoe on display during the World's Fair in New York in 1965. Photo courtesy of Barbara Langhammer.

Zach, Jr. with his father-in-law, who sold MonArk boats at his local market, circa mid-1960s.

A flat bottom jon boat with a cabin on it, the MonArk Belle was the first large boat in the company's product line.

A Legal Battle Ensues

MonArk hadn't been in business long when DuraCraft, owned by the Ward family, filed a lawsuit against them. MonArk was using the name "Fisherman" on the side of their boats, as did DuraCraft, who felt that MonArk was misrepresenting their product. The suit cost MonArk $25,000 to fight—a lot of money to the fledgling company—and nearly meant an end to their business venture. Zach recalled, "In the trial, we had all kinds of evidence to show the judge that the pattern we were building was not owned by anybody, that this design was not unique to DuraCraft. We won the lawsuit but the judge ruled that we had to quit using the word 'Fisherman' on the side of the boat."

Zach's association with the Ward family of DuraCraft Boats went back to his childhood and he acknowledges that the two families have always engaged in some friendly competition. If anything, the possibility of losing the new business only strengthened Zach's resolve to succeed as the Wards had. Both families, like many other small independent companies, experienced the sale of their business to a larger company at some point in their history. Fifty years later, Zach has the pleasure of watching his children at the helm of the business he built, and the grandchildren of the original Ward boat-builders are also still building boats in Monticello to this day.

The Air National Guard

Like his father, Zach had a natural thirst for learning. He had learned to fly with a friend he'd met at Davidson College. In an effort to further his interest in flying, Zach put his name on a list to join the Air National Guard. Zach learned to fly small planes for his company and personal use and was in the Civil Air Patrol. Perhaps more importantly, his time in the Air National Guard led to one very valuable connection. While in Biloxi, Mississippi, for summer camp in 1962, he met his future wife, Dianne. She was from Kaplan, Louisiana, and after their initial meeting, Zach had to

A young Robin McClendon at the wheel of a MonArk houseboat.

Bill Parks laughs while Joe Dean affixes brass to Zach's uniform in preparation for an ROTC drill while attending Davidson College in North Carolina.

do a lot of research to find her, thinking she'd said she was from "Cow Pen." She spoke French as her first language until she began attending school. Her family was Cajun and Zach fit in well, fully enjoying the Cajun culture that included shrimp boating, good times, and good food. Zach and Dianne were married in 1962 and Robin came along the following year.

The MonArk Crew

In 1963, MonArk bought the old Root Manufacturing plant on Patton Street, formerly a lawn mower manufacturing plant, and the MonArk family continued to grow. Monroe Stuckey was hired for marketing and sales, Larry Flemister was hired as a welder, and Herman "Curly" Fleming was the main boat-hauler. A lady named Ima Wells held down the office.

From the beginning, MonArk was blessed with hardworking and loyal employees. After a few years, Larry Flemister was put in charge of manufacturing and he recalled the tightly knit workforce of those days. Back then, some of the employees came in early and had coffee after they punched in until it was time to start work. A representative from the labor board reviewed the time cards and informed Larry that the workers would have to be paid for the extra time that was on their time cards. After discussing it with Zach, Larry brought the guys in, explained the situation and gave them the option of accepting or declining the extra pay. "Only three men took the checks," Larry recalled. "The rest of them said, 'You don't owe me that.'"

After about four years as a welder, Larry became vice president and hired his brother, Bobby Jack, to be shop foreman and manage the parts department.

Bobby Jack stayed at MonArk until the early 1970s and he and Zach have remained good friends over the years. They still meet every morning for breakfast, along with a few other friends, to solve the problems of the world over coffee. He is quick to acknowledge all that the McClendons have done over the years for the city of Monticello, regretting that they don't always get the credit they deserve. "I could call Zach, Jr. right now at midnight if I needed something and he'd be there," Bobby Jack will tell you. "You just don't find many people like him."

As for Zach, Sr., Larry recalled the time MonArk was building a houseboat for his brother, Bob McClendon. "We worked on it and worked on it and Mr. Bob kept adding this and adding that, so Mr. Zach said, 'Larry, if you will do everything you can to get this boat out of here so we can get it shipped to him down the river, I'll buy you the best Stetson hat that The Leader (a local clothing store) sells.' Well, I did my

Zach, Jr. (top, left) in Alaska, working on the railroad following his high school graduation.

best. Bill Edwards called me one day from The Leader and said, 'Larry, come on up here—I've got something for you.' I went up there and sure enough, Mr. Zach had bought me a brand new Stetson hat. He was a man of his word."

By the mid-1960s, MonArk was building 14-foot, 16-foot, and 18-foot jon boats and they were building them wider and deeper than the competition. Having learned of MonArk's increasing reputation for quality, the Arkansas Game and Fish Commission ordered a 16-foot jon boat with a cabin. Elmo Judkins designed the cabin, and MonArk built the boat, thus launching their workboat division.

MonArk's 1965 product catalog included a variety of aluminum fishing boats, semi-vee utility boats, and canoes, and featured the Pro, a shallow draft, high-speed boat with a modified-vee-type hull, as well as the *MonArk Belle*, an 18-foot version of the boat originally designed for the Arkansas Game and Fish Commission.

Double Dare

The sense of daring that Zach displayed even as a boy has remained one of his hallmark traits. Two of the stories that illustrate that daring involved airplanes.

On a trip to New Orleans with Larry Flemister, the Cessna that Zach was flying was the last plane allowed to take off from New Orleans as storms threatened the entire area. As the storm began to toss the plane (and its contents) around, Zach heard a pilot in another plane lamenting the rough weather conditions. Zach replied to him, "Yeah, we'll just have to ride this one out," to which the other pilot replied, "You're gonna need some spurs to ride this one out!" When Zach and Larry landed, they discovered that the storm had indeed destroyed part of the Monticello airport.

Another time, Zach was flying his family to South Louisiana for the Christmas holidays. Realizing that he was lost, he got out a map to regain his bearings. John was sitting up front with Zach, but being only six years old at the time, he couldn't even see over the console. Unable to hold a map and read it while he was flying, Zach said to John, "You hold the yoke right here," and proceeded to check the map to get the plan back on course. Is it any wonder that Robin and John recall their mother being a white-knuckled flyer?

Monticello Boat Manufacturer to Nearly Double Its Plant

Special to The Commercial

MONTICELLO — Plans to virtually double existing production facilities have been announced by MonArk Boat Company here.

Zach McClendon Jr., president of the eight-year old firm, said the additional room was needed to keep pace with increasing boat and camper sales but primarily to permit further diversification.

A 22,000-square-foot building will be erected parallel to the existing 27,000-square-foot boat plant, and will enable MonArk to expand its houseboat and pontoon cruiser construction. In addition, a 3,000 - square - foot building will provide one-day storage for newly finished boats.

The interior woodwork on the houseboats will be finished in MonArk's year-old Camper Division, across town. An additional 12,000-square - foot structure is being provided for this, and also for stepped-up production of travel trailers (15-foot and 18-foot mobile homes).

Don Echols, director of camp-

A 1966 Pine Bluff Commercial *article announces MonArk's plans to build a 22,000-square-foot expansion.*

Drew Foam

By 1965, the cottonseed oil mill business was declining. MonArk was in full swing and they were buying polystyrene foam from Dow Chemical for the flotation they used in their recreational boats. When one of Dow's friendlier deliverymen called on them one day, Zach, Sr. and Zach, Jr. asked him how the foam was made and he happily told them all he knew. The process caught Zach, Jr.'s interest and the two decided to try to make it themselves. "You start with a material that looks like sugar, but it's really little bubbles of polystyrene with pentane gas," he described. "When you put that under heat, the gas expands, and the bubbles get soft on the outside. It blows up like popcorn." The rest of the story is best told by Zach's son John, who has no doubt heard it and told it many times.

"They soon realized that polystyrene was thermally expanded with steam. Steam use was right down Zach, Sr.'s alley, so they decided to try and set up their own machine to make it. It's just not in Zach's nature to think that a project might be too big for him to tackle. Well, they built this God-awful contraption and shot the steam to it for the first time. It screeched and creaked for a moment and then blew apart into a thousand pieces. One of the steam fittings hit Zach, Jr. on the head and damn near killed him.

"Undeterred, they put it all back together and decided to try it once more. Voila! This time it worked. That was the beginning of Drew Foam."

Zach, Sr. closed the cottonseed oil business to manage Drew Foam. Ninety-eight percent of its sales went to flotation, and MonArk was the company's main customer. Eventually, they went to computerized equipment for foam manufacture and had additional manufacturing and distribution facilities in Memphis, Nashville, two locations in Georgia, and one very large operation in Hammond, Louisiana. The internal supply and product diversification MonArk enjoyed through their association with Drew Foam helped them through the occasional economic downturn.

Gulf Coast Oil Boom

MonArk's real entry into workboat production came with the offshore oil boom that started in the Gulf during the mid-1960s. The oil companies needed pumper boats and heavier craft capable of carrying crews out to the wells. It was here that Zach found his way into the workboat market.

The problem was, MonArk didn't have the engineers they needed to design these bigger, heavier boats, and figuring out how to install an inboard engine posed a challenge. As Zach recalled, "It was a magical thing to us as to how you could put a shaft through the bottom of a boat and line it up straight enough to tie it into the engine." Zach and Elmo went to South Louisiana and started visiting the boat-builders that were plenti-

Drew Foam Companies

Construction Products

Zach, Sr. and Zach, Jr. started up Drew Foam in 1965. This brochure from 1990 shows a sample of the architectural details the company fabricated from expanded polystyrene.

One of the first boats built for oilfield use by MonArk for the oil company market in Southern Louisiana. Zach was able to break into the market, supplying these workboats to Shell Oil and other buyers.

ful along the Gulf at the time. At Breaux Bay Craft, Zach encountered the owner, Roy Breaux, Sr., a laid-back fellow who was more than happy to share his expertise, never imagining that these two fellows from Monticello, Arkansas, might ever be competitors.

With Roy's advice under their arm, Zach and Elmo headed home and Zach began courting Shell Oil Company's business. One of the earliest demonstration boats had a glitch that made for a pretty interesting story. Having hauled the boat down to the Gulf, and with an engineer from Shell Oil present, Zach cranked up the boat only to discover that the steering lines and the hydraulic systems had been hooked up backwards. Years later, Zach paints a pretty good picture of what it was like to try to handle that boat. "So here we are in all that boat traffic in the canal, trying to steer," he said. "If you wanted to go left, the boat went right; if you wanted to go forward, the boat went in reverse. The poor Shell engineer was scared to death!" Somehow, Zach eventually managed to

get the boat and the petrified Shell engineer back to shore. With no credit established with the local parts supplier, Zach had to have Ima Wells wire him the money he needed to buy the parts to fix the boat. Zach must have won their confidence because Shell ended up accepting delivery of the boat and the crew boats and pumpers required by the oil industry went on to become a major product line for MonArk.

Arkansas Corps of Engineers

MonArk's first really big contract came a few years later from the Corps of Engineers. The Arkansas River Development project was nearing completion and the Corps of Engineers put out a bid for five 30-foot boats to be used for weekly inspections of the seven dams. Zach remembers well the day he went to Little Rock for the bid opening and when he found out MonArk was the low bidder, he was taken a bit by surprise. "I was wondering," he said, "what the hell have we gotten ourselves into?" The first of the five boats was delivered to the city of Dumas, Arkansas, in July 1968 equipped with a Raytheon Depth Recorder for making hydrographic surveys. However challenging some of these early projects proved to be, they gave MonArk the assurance they needed to become a serious player in the workboat business.

Branching Out

Zach's love of houseboats goes back to his childhood and is perhaps rooted in his love for the water. It's only logical that if you love the water that much, then living on it must be the best way to go. That's why, as soon as Zach was able, he added houseboats to MonArk's product line. MonArk's five houseboat models ranged from the modest family-style craft to the luxurious 60-foot version capable of sleeping twelve people in comfort.

Always looking for new markets for their boats, MonArk purchased the maritime division of Alliance Machine Company of Ohio in 1968. This was the beginning of MonArk's aluminum cathedral hull boat. The Mariner series was a line of all-welded aluminum inboard/outboard, utility, and workboats in 17-foot, 19-foot, and 21-foot lengths. The cathedral hull offered increased stability in rough water.

Interestingly enough, though the cathedral hull design was originally purchased to be a recreational product, it didn't get an enthusiastic response from recreational boat dealers. It did, however, become one of the most popular designs for the workboat division and now SeaArk Marine, particularly for customers who require a very stable work platform, as in hydrographic survey work. Zach's willingness to explore a design or product and then adapt it to another application when necessary laid the foundation for the breadth of design capability that SeaArk now offers its customers.

In 1969, Zach made the decision to branch out into fiberglass boat production. It was the beginning of the fiberglass fishing boat market, a flashier, more exciting and versatile product line than the traditional jon boats, though they posed some challenges. MonArk didn't have the engineering they needed to credibly enter this new product line, but that wasn't enough to deter Zach from a product that had caught his imagination and fired up his enthusiasm.

Though necessary to some degree, MonArk's product diversification challenged their production and management capabilities. By then, their product line included a complete line of aluminum recreational boats including flat bottoms, four models of canoes, semi-vee utility boats, pontoon cruisers, and houseboats. But because Zach was well acquainted with the sportsman's needs, they were also manufacturing aluminum ice chests, camper tops, toolboxes, deer stands, and fuel tanks.

Ultimately, the fiberglass boat business was instrumental in elevating MonArk as a major competitor among boat builders. Many of the fiberglass models

A MonArk houseboat, circa 1971.

Entrepreneurial Excess

Truth be told, some of the "extra" products that MonArk manufactured in its early years conveniently accommodated some of Zach's own hobbies, but they also came from his first-hand knowledge about what hunters and fishermen are looking for. Today's plastic ice chests weren't available then, so the choices were either the flimsy foam variety or the big heavy steel chests. MonArk's aluminum ice chests were insulated with Drew Foam's expanded polystyrene and had a cushion on top to provide additional seating on the boat. They were a favorite among dealers. Camper tops, designed to turn virtually any pick-up into a mobile hunting lodge, were introduced in the mid-1960s. When Zach told Ron Echols he wanted to start manufacturing camper tops, Ron's reply was, "Great! What's a camper top?"

Tool boxes and fuel tanks were basic equipment and the aluminum deer stands, portable

and lightweight, were actually ahead of their time. A simple ladder-type stand, they were eight to ten feet tall with a two-by-two-foot platform at the top. But from here, the list gets just a little stranger. First there were the beanbag chairs, a very popular item for a few years. The upholstery person from the boat company sewed the vinyl bags and they were filled with the beads left over from polystyrene foam manufacture.

Then there was the monster known as the Mud Hog Track Vehicle. Built at one of Zach's numerous side companies, Zach developed it as an all-terrain vehicle after observing how many of the oil company crews had to slog their way through swamps in Central and South America. Only one was ever built. As John said, "The oil companies looked at it and said, 'What the hell is this?' The tracks were so loud you couldn't sit in it and it vibrated so they brought it back and put rubber inserts in the tracks." It was used only once when Zach took John for a ride on the ice-covered streets of Monticello during a winter storm and then sold to a guy in Oklahoma who had a business cleaning sewer ponds.

One summer John came home from college to work at Drew Foam and Zach presented him with his latest idea—he was going to make foam doghouses. One piece of polystyrene foam was laminated with two pieces of rigid vinyl for the sides. Notches were cut so the thing could

The MonArk Mud Hog was designed in 1982 with South American oil crews in mind, but it never made it past the original prototype, which was manufactured at E M & F, one of Zach McClendon's side ventures.

The aluminum chemical tank and the tool chest were just two of MonArk's diversified products during the late 1960s.

be folded and thus made ship-able. John's job was to use the hot wire to cut the foam. "There's no telling how many of those things I made that summer," he said, "and I bet they didn't sell five of them."

Zach had another idea that became a Drew Foam product in the mid-90s—foam mailboxes. Under the company name "Earthworks," and with the help of Drew Foam employees, he developed a series of arched blocks about three feet tall, which were cut from foam and then coated with cement. A standard mailbox was then inserted in the top part of the block. The colored cement was stamped with a brick or stone pattern and the finished product looked surprisingly realistic. Options included an opening in the back of the mailbox for large packages and some had Japanese-style "roofs." Zach's intention was to sell the mailboxes through hardware stores to homeowners who wanted a "brick" mailbox at the end of their driveway. Although the product was great, the distribution chain never developed and it didn't take off as planned. However, Zach uses his own foam mailbox to this day!

Aluminum ice chests, deer stands, and camper tops were among MonArk's secondary product line.

This sleek cruiser built in 1968 was at that time the largest conventional hull aluminum craft ever constructed in Arkansas. The 58-foot vessel had a cruising range of 1,200 miles, radar, and advanced electronic equipment along with sleeping, living, cooking, and dining facilities.

were very popular and with the wide array of models available in both aluminum and fiberglass, boat dealers could have a full line with just the MonArk brand including jon boats, ski boats, canoes, sailboats, houseboats, and pontoon boats. The fiberglass side of the business helped to build the dealer base, establish the MonArk name as a major player in the boat-building business, and helped the company grow. As evidence that the MonArk name was picking up speed, an ad featured in the April 13, 1969 edition of the *Arkansas Gazette* listed forty-three dealers in Arkansas alone!

MonArk's Bread and Butter

Looking back, it's clear that MonArk's diverse product line truly turned out to be a double-edged sword. While causing considerable headaches at times, and some challenging manufacturing issues, it was also this diversity that helped establish the company's name and carry it through some lean times.

Johnny Smith, who worked for MonArk from early 1972 to 1993, still contends that their best product in those early years was "the plain old simple aluminum

Duck Hunting Costa Rica-style

When Zach started an aluminum boat business in Costa Rica with Roberto Chavez, Larry Flemister accompanied him on one of the early trips. Knowing they were avid duck hunters, Roberto invited Zach and Larry to go hunting with him and his friends.

When they heard the duck hunting site was sixty miles away, they figured that wouldn't be a bad drive. That didn't turn out to be the case. It took six of them squashed together cheek-by-jowl in a Land Rover eight hours to make the trip. When they arrived, they saw a big plantation surrounded by rice fields and thought they had the whole place to themselves. That didn't turn out to be the case either. Larry recalled, "Come to find out, when we pulled up, there was an airplane landing on the airstrip. The man who owned the plantation decided to fly in that weekend with all his folks and they were staying at the house!" Relegated to sleeping out in the rice fields, Larry said, "We had to sleep under the truck; the mosquitoes were so bad they would eat you up and it was hot." Larry wasn't impressed with the hunting either. "You had to wade in the water to about waist deep with leeches all over the place," he said. With disdain evident in his voice, he said, "When the ducks came in we shot 'em, but they weren't nothin' but coots! That's what they called a duck."

boat," and it remains the company's bread and butter. The jon boats built by SeaArk Boats today are much bigger and heavier than the early boats, and offer the customer a phenomenal array of options and features.

Aluminum Boats of Costa Rica

As the 1960s drew to a close, a fellow named Roberto Chavez, whose family was in the export/import business in San Jose, contacted Zach about entering the

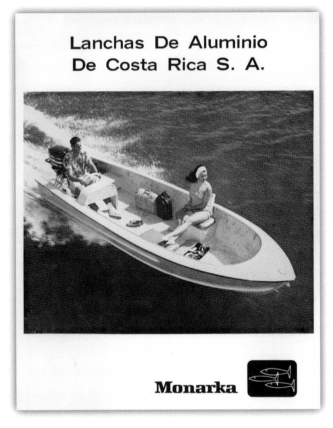

boat business. Zach discussed it with Zach, Sr. and they decided to pursue it. Eager to learn, Roberto stayed in Monticello for a couple of months, visiting the plant every day. The operation only lasted a couple of years and produced more good stories than profit. Zach and Larry Flemister went to Costa Rica to set up some of the equipment and found some innovative ways of handling the language barrier. They painted drills different colors for different-sized bits and then instructed the workers as to which color should be drilled where. Roberto, who Zach described as "a big, nice-looking guy with a wonderful personality who should have been a politician," recruited a work force that Zach had to instruct to show up for work "when the sun came up." Apparently they didn't catch on to Zach's hand motions because Larry recalled them arriving at ten o'clock, quitting at noon and coming back at two, and then leaving again at three o'clock for siesta. As Larry said, "It's hard to build a lot of boats when you only work three hours a day."

Roberto Chavez turned out to be another one of those dabblers and dreamers that Zach has attracted throughout his career. What's worth noting is that it was Roberto who found Zach instead of the other way around, which means that MonArk's reputation had traveled as far away as Central America.

A brochure for Aluminum Boats of Costa Rica.

Larry Flemister (left) of MonArk and Roberto Chavez in front of the manufacturing facility of Aluminum Boats of Costa Rica, 1969.

MonArk® boats

MONTICELLO, ARKANSAS

ALUMINUM FISHING BOAT DIVISION
1976

- SEMI-VEES
- CANOES
- FLATBOTTOMS

14' semi-V (3025). ▲

17' canoe (4026). ▲

14' flatbottom (1465). ▼

1976 MonArk catalog cover.

Chapter Three

MONARK MAKES A NAME FOR ITSELF

As the 1960s wound to a close, things at MonArk were going well. Reaping the benefits of the offshore oil boom, the workboat division was beginning to take root.

However, the economy was growing lukewarm and the oil boom was showing signs of coming to a halt. To make matters worse, things were literally about to go up in flames.

Fire Strikes

The path to success seldom moves in a straight line, no matter how determined the entrepreneur, and Zach McClendon is no ordinary entrepreneur. In fact, adversity only seems to fuel his determination. So it was when fire destroyed MonArk's fiberglass plant in May 1971. The building had been expanded to 20,000 square feet just the year before after only a year of production. Black smoke billowed skyward as fiberglass resin and barrels of acetone exploded to create an inferno. The cause of the fire was never determined, but the intensity of the heat created by various chemicals and plastics used in production caused the structure's steel beams to collapse, resulting in a total loss of the fiberglass facility, a loss that Zach McClendon placed somewhere near $100,000. Striking in the middle of MonArk's peak production period, the fire precluded any further shipment of the company's 1971 fiberglass models.

Though Zach could only watch helplessly when he arrived at the plant that morning to see it going up in flames, by the time local newspaper reporters interviewed him he was already announcing plans to rebuild the plant to twice the size of the original. The new plant opened the following September, more than double its original size, with employment increased from forty-four to one hundred, in time to begin production of the 1972 line of fiberglass boats.

The slumping economy and the fire in the fiberglass plant combined to diminish MonArk's profitability in 1971, even as sales volume continued to rise. While houseboat sales were sluggish, pontoon cruisers, classic runabouts, and utility boats showed strong gains even into 1972 and the company's basic aluminum fishing boats, a mainstay for the company, continued to set new sales records.

This 1970 sales photo displays the wide variety of products the company had developed.

Zach and his sister, Paddy, relax with their father, Zach McClendon, Sr., on a MonArk houseboat on the Arkansas River, circa 1970.

Zach (third from left) looks on as MonArk's fiberglass plant burns in May 1971. Larry Flemister (second from right) tries to console him. Photo courtesy of the Advance Monticellonian.

A view of the MonArk Workboat Division shows the combination of Zach, Sr.'s converted cottonseed buildings and new shops specifically for boat-building.

Zach speaks during the christening ceremony for MonArk Shipyard's first-ever towboat, while Bob C. Riley (with eyepatch), lieutenant governor for the state of Arkansas, and Zach, Sr. (second from right) look on, circa 1971.

Thinking BIG

Sales in the oilfield market were declining as a result of the oil crisis that was looming on the horizon by 1972. While most business owners might pull in the reins at such market indications, Zach headed into it full force like a linebacker braced for the tackle. Two of Zach's most endearing (and challenging) traits were at play here: his ability to dream big and his vulnerability to those who are capable of dreaming as big as he does.

"I'd had it in my mind ever since I had been running around South Louisiana that for us to really get into big boats we had to be on the water," Zach explained. "The Arkansas River had just been made navigable all the

The MV Christine, *MonArk Shipyard's first workboat, was launched in June 1972. Photo courtesy of the* Advance Monticellonian.

way to Tulsa. I had always wanted to build bigger boats and this seemed like the perfect opportunity." He hired a man named Ed Fry who had many years of experience in steel boat construction in Alton, Illinois. No buildings were needed since the barges, towboats, and other large boats Zach had in mind to manufacture were too large to be contained by four walls. Plans were made to build a variety of floating all-steel vessels ranging in size up to 300 feet in length and 400 tons gross weight. With a goal of building the five steel boats a year it would take to be profitable, Zach started MonArk Shipyards in Pine Bluff as a subsidiary to MonArk Boat Company. In less than a year, MonArk Shipyards started work on a total of twelve boats and had orders for seventeen more.

The shipyard in Pine Bluff was an historic first. The first shipyard in Arkansas, it was located on forty acres on the south bank of the Boyd's Point cutoff of the redeveloped Arkansas River, the nation's largest inland waterway system. Its first launching

was in June 1972—a 22-foot-wide, 56-foot-long, 75-ton towboat named the *MV Christine*, the first commercial towboat produced in Arkansas. It was built for Ike Carter of the Carter Construction Company of Benton for construction and maintenance projects on the Arkansas River and its tributaries.

In early 1973, MonArk Shipyards celebrated its first anniversary by delivering its fifth and largest self-propelled vessel. A 75-foot oceanographic research vessel built for use by the U.S. Navy Underwater Systems Command at Newport, Rhode Island, it included a decompression chamber and special heavy lift capabilities for deep-water diving. Competing against proposals from several builders, MonArk Shipyards won the contract based on design, delivery time, and price. Dubbed the *Sea Horse*, the boat gave MonArk its entry to the military boat business.

While most people would be satisfied to realize one good idea at a time, Zach McClendon suffers from no such constraints. Ed encouraged Zach to team up with a couple of struggling boat builders in South Louisiana. As a result, MonArk Custom Craft was started up in Jeanerette, Louisiana. The aluminum vessels manufactured there, up to 125 feet in length, were intended for offshore and commercial purposes.

MonArk Custom Craft in Louisiana was building a product called SuperCat, a 75-foot-long catamaran. Referred to as head boats, they were used to take a hundred or so fishermen at a time, equipped with their own gear and charged "by the head," out to

The SuperCat, built by the Custom Craft Division of MonArk Boat Company.

A jo boat (pumper boat) bound for oilfield service work going through the decking stage of welding during the early 1970s.

a fishing spot for the day. In addition to head boats, Custom Craft was also building some crew boats for the offshore oil industry.

Unfortunately, neither of these companies was as successful financially as they were technically. Custom Craft was sold to an investment group out of Maryland headed by a fellow who had his heart set on building aluminum catamarans. MonArk Shipyards in Pine Bluff was also sold and under its new ownership became Steelship.

Back to Basics

With the sale of MonArk Shipyards and Custom Craft, Zach was able to return to focus on boat production in Monticello. MonArk's plan for garnering a larger share of the recreational boat market was to give their products added value and customer appeal through increased accessory items including a ten-speed electric trolling motor and a lightweight fish-finder calibrated for one-hundred-foot readings. MonArk's program for

product diversification found them projecting a banner year for 1972–1973 and earned them rights to the title of "the world's most diversified boat builder."

In contrast, Ron Echols, who had joined the company back in 1965, felt that the product lines had become too diversified to be profitable. From Ron's viewpoint, they were "trying to do too many things for too many people with not enough engineering on the front end." As if to give fuel to Ron's argument, in 1972 Alcoa, who was MonArk's primary supplier of aluminum for the boats, ice chests, tool boxes, camper tops, and deer stands they were manufacturing, put the entire industry on allocation due to the energy crisis, forcing MonArk to limit its product lines. Zach named Ron Echols vice president in charge of manufacturing with special emphasis on production efficiency and quality control.

Taking the bull by the horns, Ron convinced Zach to trim down MonArk's product line: pontoons, ice chests, tool boxes, and semi-vees went by the wayside and the

Lunker Busters

VOL. 1—NO. 4   NOVEMBER-DECEMBER, 1972

LUNKER BUSTERS AT MILLWOOD

Cover of the Lunker Busters *magazine, November/December 1972.*

Lunker Busters

When Bassmaster Magazine came out in 1968, MonArk purchased the inside cover space to advertise their bass boats. They weren't exactly taken seriously, though, and found themselves bumped off the advertising roster with the next edition. Ron Werth of Faulkner Advertising in Pine Bluff was handling MonArk's marketing and came up with the idea of starting their own club, complete with a magazine, to ease the sting of Bassmaster's rejection. The idea was to appeal to a broader base of fishermen and promote jon boats and other recreational boats as well as bass boats. Mr. Werth made an enthusiastic presentation announcing his idea for the name of the club: Lunker Busters. Ron Echols didn't like the name but Zach loved it, so Lunker Busters it was. Ron Werth became the editor of Lunker Busters magazine, and within a year, the club's membership included anglers from thirty-six states. The club's first tournament was held in November 1973 at Millwood Lake, Arkansas. Prizes included a 1973 MonArk Super Sport, a Delta III, and the new Bass Special, with $250 going to the fishermen who landed the largest bass on each day of the competition.

In 1975, MonArk designed and built this boat for Shell Oil Company for searching for offshore oil deposits off Prudhoe Bay, Alaska.

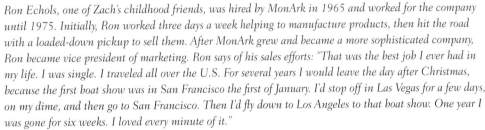

Ron Echols, one of Zach's childhood friends, was hired by MonArk in 1965 and worked for the company until 1975. Initially, Ron worked three days a week helping to manufacture products, then hit the road with a loaded-down pickup to sell them. After MonArk grew and became a more sophisticated company, Ron became vice president of marketing. Ron says of his sales efforts: "That was the best job I ever had in my life. I was single. I traveled all over the U.S. For several years I would leave the day after Christmas, because the first boat show was in San Francisco the first of January. I'd stop off in Las Vegas for a few days, on my dime, and then go to San Francisco. Then I'd fly down to Los Angeles to that boat show. One year I was gone for six weeks. I loved every minute of it."

number of flat bottom boat styles was cut by at least half.

Ron hired a design firm out of Chicago to design a boat that, according to Ron, "was very successful and set the trend for years to come." It was a multi-purpose boat that could be used for fishing, skiing, or just taking the family out for an afternoon called the Super Sport.

Ron credits the company's turnaround to the widespread popularity of bass boats of which MonArk was one of the very first developers. Bass fishermen are very serious about their sport and demand that their boats be rigged to do nothing else. To satisfy them, a boat has to be fast, especially for tournament fishing, since every minute spent going from one spot to another is time spent with your line out of the water. They also require at least one live well (two was even better) deep enough to keep the fish alive. Finally, the boats had to have rod lockers to secure their fishing gear.

18,000 Boats

In 1973, MonArk entered into an agreement with Berman Leasing Company out of Englewood, New Jersey, for the leasing of twenty International Harvester highway tractors and twenty boat trailers for making deliveries to

more than 750 MonArk dealers across the country. By this time, MonArk was being touted as one of the fastest-growing recreational and workboat builders in the world. The transportation equipment was used to deliver MonArk's 1973 production of an estimated 18,000 boats.

MonArk's 1974 lineup provided some clearly distinct differences in each of the company's twenty-one different models. Marketing research had indicated that certain duplications in MonArk's designs were confusing to customers. As a result, the line was reduced in 1974 to include six lengths of flat bottoms ranging from 10 feet to 20 feet, all featuring gas-resistant foam flotation. Included were five Coast Guard-approved rescue boats and eight commercial fishing boats. Wanting to please the serious fisherman whose needs Zach understood so well, the "Bass Special" was designed to let the fisherman customize the interior and accessories to suit his individual needs.

The Bank of West Memphis and Union Bank of Monticello

Despite an already hectic schedule, Zach ventured into another area of business, one that he'd had his eye on for quite some time. Firmly entrenched in Monticello's commerce, Zach and his father both held Union Bank of

MonArk's 1973 fiberglass sport fishing boats, bottom to top: Super Pro Ltd., Riviera IV, Mark II, Delta Target, and Delta II.

MonArk's new 15-foot, 2-inch Delta III fiberglass boat, 1973.

MonArk's new flat bottom model 1431, 1973.

A 1973 press release announced "Three new products from MonArk Accessories Division": live well, improved steering console, and seat brackets.

Monticello in tremendous esteem and felt that someday owning a part of it would be a great honor. However, the bank's ownership appeared to be locked up by another prominent family of Monticello, so those dreams were put on the back burner—for the time being.

Then one day in 1973, a business broker called on Zach and attempted to interest him in a couple of boat businesses. Zach convinced him he wasn't interested, but on the way out the door the broker glanced back and said, "You wouldn't be interested in buying a bank, would you?" Zach waved the fellow back in the door and learned that the Bank of West Memphis was up for sale. He took the idea to his father and upon hearing it would be a $2.4-million deal, Zach, Sr. responded, "We can't do that." Once again undaunted, Zach encouraged his father to accompany him to Little Rock to talk to some bankers with whom he was well acquainted. Zach recalled that his father kept repeating, "I don't know why I'm wasting my time. We can't do this deal," all the way to Little Rock.

As it turned out, state banking regulations at the time prohibited a bank from having branches in any county other than the one in which they were chartered. Knowing there was legislation on the table to change

This photo, taken at the groundbreaking for the Union Bank and Trust building expansion, appeared in the Advance Monticellonian *in 1972. Zach, Sr. (second from left) was chairman of the board at the time. Photo courtesy of the* Advance Monticellonian.

that, a plan was devised whereby the McClendons would purchase the Bank of West Memphis with the intention of selling it to Worthen Bank as a branch once the legislation was passed. Zach described it as "a two-year plan that turned into a six-year plan." As usual, the legislation took longer to pass than anticipated; however, with Zach's leadership, the bank was a successful business venture for the McClendons. Eventually it provided them with the means to become part owners of Union Bank in Monticello.

At the same time that Zach, Jr. was overseeing the Bank of West Memphis, Zach, Sr. had been given the honor of being named Chairman of the Board of Union Bank in Monticello. Union Bank was facing some rather stiff competition from another local bank. When a member of the Union Bank Board suggested that Zach, Jr. be offered the job as bank president in 1976, he accepted the position, and over the next five years, Union Bank made tremendous gains on the competition. It is worth noting that the McClendons' eventual sale of the Bank of West Memphis was to the Dunklin family, who were also in the cottonseed oil mill business.

Whether or not things worked out exactly as anticipated, what is worth noting is the strength of Zach McClendon, Jr.'s vision and his ability to think strategically years in advance in order to achieve that vision. Zach, Sr. once said to his son, "Sonny, your ability to generate deals is faster than I can find the money to back them up!" That level of trust and confidence in his son's abilities would be repeated someday as Zach, Jr. turned over the helm to yet another generation.

Conquering whitewater in a durable 17-foot MonArk aluminum canoe, 1973.

The People of MonArk

All of the McClendons—Zach, Robin, and John—are quick to acknowledge all the people who have worked with them over the years to help them build a successful business. Most of MonArk's earliest employees were longtime friends of Zach and his family. Ron Echols knew Zach from their Boy Scout years, saying,

"Zach had more energy than anyone I've ever known and he was able to transform that energy into leadership." Ron quickly took a leadership role himself at MonArk. Realizing that they had some workforce-related challenges, Ron convinced Zach to institute some improved employee benefits, primarily for the purpose of giving them some leverage against that nemesis of small

Three of MonArk's semi-vees, early 1970s. From top: 16-foot whitewater model 3045, 16-foot model 3029, and 14-foot model 3012.

MonArk built sailboats in the 1970s. This M-1 model was a 14-foot craft with two seven-foot compartments for stowing gear and oars, and six smaller storage spaces. Though sleek and elegant, sailboats never became a successful addition to the company's product line. Courtesy of SeaArk.

business-owners throughout Arkansas—deerhunters. "People would literally quit their jobs to go deer hunting," Ron recalled.

Dick Dickinson joined the MonArk sales force in 1972 and remembers their major sales point being the quality and service upon which Zach had built the company's reputation. "We had a real tight-knit group of sales people who supported and helped each other," Dick said, "and we had very, very loyal dealers. To have a MonArk dealership, you had to be one of the top dealers in that particular area."

Dick Dickinson had a long and illustrious career with MonArk, working several different territories. After several moves, Dick accepted the position of Vice President of Sales, which came with the added bonus of being able to move back to his hometown of Monticello. In 1982, though, he gave up his vice presidential title to work the Texas/Louisiana territory when it opened up and quickly became the company's first "Two-Million-Dollar Salesperson."

Being a salesman for MonArk required a tremendous amount of product knowledge, including the competition's products. And sometimes, they were called on to do some spur-of-the-moment trouble-shooting. Dick recalled the time a dealer in St. Louis called him about the 10-foot and 12-foot aluminum boats he was having trouble selling, assuming they were too small to appeal to his customers. Dick visited the dealer and discovered that he had the boats stacked upside down, giving them the illusion of being smaller than they were. Dick suggested they take one boat of each size and stand them up against the building. A couple weeks later, the dealer called Dick and said, "Boy, you hit the nail on the head! Send me another twenty more of each!"

By 1974, the Bank of West Memphis and Drew Foam were demanding a great deal of Zach's time and energy. Feeling he was spread too thin to do justice to the operations at MonArk, Zach hired Bob Lee that August to take the helm as president of MonArk. For the next ten years, Bob oversaw both the workboat and recreational boat divisions.

MonArk has truly been blessed with its share of loyal employees and the memory of one in particular is rather bittersweet—Bill Grant. Bill was a salesman for the workboat division of MonArk who was, by all admissions, a hysterically funny guy who loved playing practical jokes on people. "You might come in to work one day and discover that your desk drawer had been turned upside down so when you opened it, everything fell on the floor," Robin McClendon recalled, also remembering the time Bill superglued her paperclip holder to the center of the top of her desk.

Dick and Gloria Dickinson, circa 1976.

Celebrity Sells

Manufacturers were using celebrities to endorse and sell their products long before the first Olympian appeared on a box of Wheaties. MonArk is no exception.

Roscoe Vernon "Gadabout" Gaddis was a veteran of professional fishing and became a spokesperson for MonArk Boats in the early 1970s. He starred on Outdoors with Liberty Mutual, *a weekly show that started as early as 1939, instilling his love for nature in a generation of youngsters who were drawn to his grandfatherly demeanor. The star of his own television show,* Flying Fisherman, *Gadabout's photo appeared in MonArk's 1972 catalog and he was quoted as saying, "MonArk really knows what this thing called fishing is all about—and they have a knack for building the kind of boats fishermen want."*

In 1974, MonArk sponsored tournament pros Jimmy Houston and Bill Norman, who became famous for his lure manufacturing. Jimmy Houston, one of the hottest fishermen in the market in 1976, was a salesman for MonArk at the same time the company was sponsoring him.

Country music star Charlie Rich visited MonArk's facilities in Monticello in 1975 and Zach presented him with a Silver Fox bass boat. Painted in striking silver metal flake, it was a luxury bass boat and the two of them, Charlie and his Silver Fox, must have been a sight to behold!

One of SeaArk's legendary stories is of the time Johnny Smith was in the conference room at SeaArk when Bill Grant came up behind him and began a rather lewd gesture. Familiar with Bill's brand of comedy, Johnny continued looking through files, barely acknowledging Bill's presence. Within a moment, Zach walked by, peeked his head in the room and simply said, "When you boys get done, I need to see you."

There's no question that Zach McClendon himself is a bit eccentric and, in return, eccentricities are accepted at SeaArk provided the source is someone who's willing to work as hard as the McClendon work ethic requires. Bill Grant certainly fit into that category, starting in the supply room at MonArk in 1967. He fought a long fight with cancer and remained with the company until his death in 1993. A plaque bearing his photo still hangs in the lobby of SeaArk Marine in his memory.

In the 1970s, a tradition was started at MonArk that has survived even to this day, though its demeanor has changed a bit over time. As a token of their appreciation for MonArk's employees, Zach started holding

Professional bass fisherman Jimmy Houston, who was sponsored by MonArk during the 1970s, appears in a promotional photo for a McFast 17, circa 1976.

This aerial view shows MonArk's expansive Recreational Division production facility in Monticello during the 1970s.

annual fishing tournaments and picnics. In the early years, the emphasis was on the fishing tournament, though the picnics generated their share of stories as well. Robin remembers the time that she and John went to one of the picnics with their mother. Dianne helped the children out of the truck, turned around only to see two guys brawling, and immediately put the children back in the truck and went home. As Zach admitted, "We had some pretty salty guys back then." Nowadays the events are more family-oriented with kid's games, prizes, and lots of barbeque. The liquid refreshments have changed as well but the message is still the same: "Thanks for a job well done."

Appreciation wasn't just limited to the employees, however. Incentive packages were offered to dealers who generated a certain volume of business. Between 1977 and 1987, locations like Acapulco, the Bahamas, the Caribbean, and Lake Tahoe were destinations for MonArk's dealer incentive trips.

Recreational Boats

Being an avid fisherman himself, Zach understood how particular boat owners could be and that one of the pleasures of boat ownership was being able to choose the options they wanted. To that end, they made it possible for customers to choose a basic design and then add their preferred options. In 1973, MonArk's Accessories Division added new products: independent live wells with aerators, improved steering console for semi-vee models, flat bottoms, and modified-vee models, and seat brackets for use in mounting swivel seats on semi-vee boats. As Ron Echols said, "We'll sell everything from anchors to zebra skin boat cushions." That same year, they introduced the Super Pro Ltd., a boat they called "the ultimate fishing machine." Looking to strengthen MonArk's position in the Pacific Northwest and Alaskan markets, they introduced the "Whitewater" boat line, a combination of a flat bottom hull with a semi-vee bow.

The McFast 15 fiberglass bass boat.

By 1974, MonArk had worked the engineering kinks out of its fiberglass boat production and they were highly popular. Virtually unlimited in their design possibilities, fiberglass boats sent Zach's imagination into hyperdrive.

It was no wonder then that MonArk was beginning to dominate the recreational boat business. Their ten models included three Delta models for all-around use, the Target for really serious fishermen, two economy-sized models, the deluxe 16-foot, 4-inch Super Sport and Super Pro for tournament fishing and family use, and two Marauder models which were, as Zach described them, "the largest, most luxurious fiberglass boats MonArk has manufactured."

MonArk's biggest success in the fiberglass boat line was the McFast, which was introduced in 1975. It was a four-point hydro-tunnel hull fishing machine with an air-suspension ride designed to "take the chop out of the water," according to a company catalog. Previously hesitant to name a boat for himself, Dick Dickinson recalled that Zach uncharacteristically announced, "This is going to be an exceptionally fast boat, seven is my lucky number, and my name starts with 'Mc,' so we're going to name the boat the McFast 7." Three models of the McFast were offered in 14-foot and 15-foot lengths. The name turned out to be pure magic and according to Dick Dickinson, "It was probably the hottest name in the market at that time." Zach said, "Our dealers told us that people would walk in to their place and say, 'I want a McFast!'" The fiberglass side of the business may not have been a financial success, but MonArk's fiberglass boats were wildly popular and in high demand at the time.

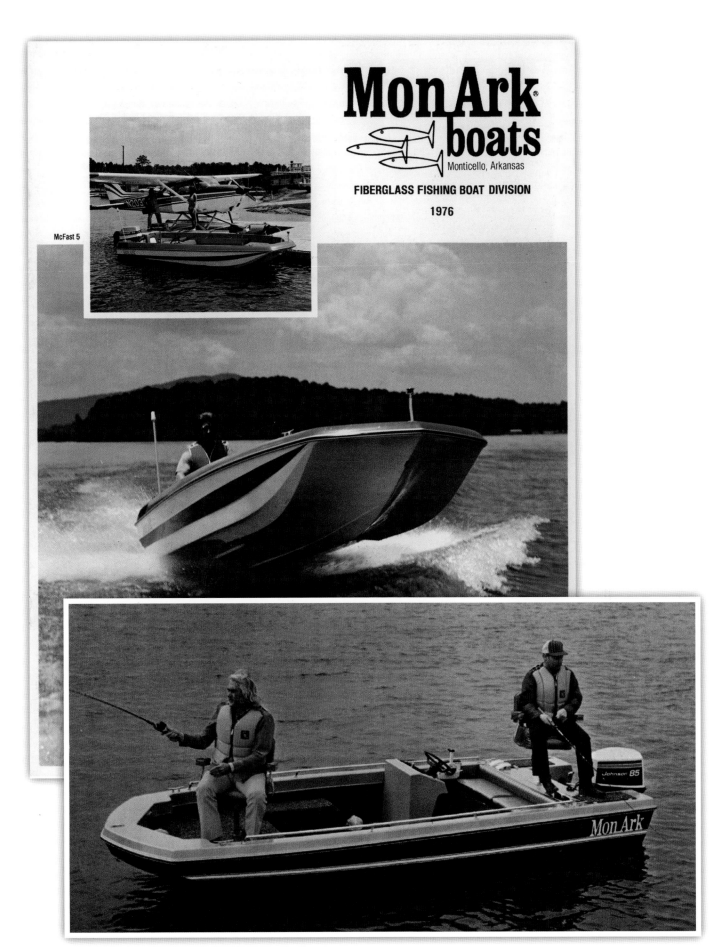

MonArk® boats
Monticello, Arkansas

FIBERGLASS FISHING BOAT DIVISION

1976

McFast 5

In a photograph from a page in this 1976 MonArk catalog, Zach (right) and country music star Charlie Rich
try out a MonArk boat model named after Rich. The Silver Fox model was produced in Monticello. Rich, who was born
in Colt, Arkansas, toured the plant and joined Zach on this test run before trailering his boat home to Memphis.

Shell Oil Company

MonArk's venture into the workboat business began with Shell Oil in the 1960s and the relationship continued for many years. In 1975, MonArk engineers designed and built a boat designed for use by scientists searching for offshore oil deposits. Shell Oil officials ordered the boat when they learned that the Alaska Lands Division was planning to lease offshore property for development the next year.

Built in prefabricated modules, it was hauled by truck to Galveston, Texas, where it was assembled and tested. It was then disassembled, loaded onto eight cargo planes, and flown 3,500 miles from Galveston, Texas, to Alaska, where it was reassembled and launched in the cold waters of Prudhoe Bay. Measuring 78 feet long by 21 feet wide, the boat could house sixteen crewmembers and carry all the seismographic equipment necessary to detect oil deposits.

Frank Fletcher, MonArk's general manager at the time, said the boat was designed and built in only six weeks for a Denver firm representing the oil company. Frank said, "As far as I know, no other company has ever built anything like this."

As the 1980s Approached

MonArk's 1975 financial report discussed the unstable economy in the U.S. that was causing a downturn in the boating industry, though they remained fairly optimistic for the coming year. By 1977, MonArk's two divisions were clearly defined. The Recreational Division was manufacturing both aluminum and fiberglass fishing boats. The aluminum fishing boat product line consisted of canoes, flat bottom jon boats, semi-vees, modified-vees, and a special line of aluminum bass boats. The fiberglass product line served the bass fishing market with up-to-date products including high-performance models. The Workboat Division's product line included all-welded aluminum boats from 17 to 40 feet for a wide range of uses as patrol boats, crew boats, utility boats, and custom-built boats. Despite an increase in sales for 1977, earnings per share dropped, but management still projected an increase in both sales and profit for 1978, the year in which MonArk's fiberglass model V-16 held the world speed record for its class with driver Bill Holland in command.

The 1979 dealer brochure announced a major change in regulations regarding boat construction.

Welcome to Nigeria!

Zach's travels on MonArk's behalf took him to places that he probably never imagined seeing while he was growing up in peaceful Monticello, Arkansas. "Between John and I, we've been all over the world. I've been all up and down Central America, I actually had a boat partnership in Costa Rica at one time, I've been to Brunei..." Zach will tell you, and then stop midstream to tell the story of the trip that, for good reason, sticks in his mind more than most.

It was 1972, and Shell Oil Company was MonArk's biggest customer by far. That was when Zach flew to Lagos, Nigeria, to meet with representatives from Shell Oil to discuss their future needs. Upon his arrival, the folks from Shell who had agreed to meet him and assist him through customs were nowhere to be found. Though the oil boom of the 1970s led to a period of prosperity for Nigeria, the civil war of previous decades had not yet translated into an orderly democracy, a fact that was not lost on Zach McClendon.

Zach found himself facing the Nigerian authorities without escort when one of the customs agents demanded that Zach follow him to another room for questioning. Zach recalls the frightening confrontation: "They took me back there in a small room with a bare light bulb hanging down and began to question me. 'Why are you here?' they asked. I told them I was there to work on some boats, but they insisted, 'No! No! Why are you here? Why are you here?'" At one point in the questioning, they even accused Zach of being a CIA operative.

"This was about nine or ten in the morning," he continued. "Finally, by about four in the afternoon, they said, 'Well, we'll have to put you in jail tonight and deport you out of the country tomorrow.' I knew they only had one flight in and out of there every day. I was too naïve to understand that what they wanted was money. Finally, one of them came into the room and I had a one-hundred-dollar bill in my hand. I gave him the one hundred dollars and he went out and I thought, 'Hell, this might be the end.' They all came back in smiling and patted me on the back. 'Everything is okay now,' they said. 'You can go.'"

Later on, the same group of fellows stole all of Zach's belongings from his hotel room. However, Zach managed to return with some real African treasures, including an ivory armband and a bronze bracelet, both of which were used as tribal currency.

Coast Guard regulations and the Boating Industry Association's certification required that level flotation would become mandatory on 1979 model year boats manufactured on or after August 1, 1978. Level flotation became a mandatory federal standard that ap-

The state of Florida purchased several of these shallow draft vessels with a steel hull shaped like a towboat. The DOT used them to clear hydrilla algae from waterways. These boats are still in use.

A promotional photo displaying MonArk's 1644V Aluminum Bass Boat from the late 1970s.

plied to outboard boats over two horsepower and less than 20 feet in length except for canoes. The increased standard provided additional stability to keep the boat afloat if swamped in calm water. As a result, MonArk discontinued some of its boats from the product line, including all Super Sport and Delta models, since the increased flotation reduced the interior area too much. It was a small adjustment for MonArk to make considering their commitment to quality and, above all, safety for the thousands of fishermen and families who relied on MonArk for their recreation.

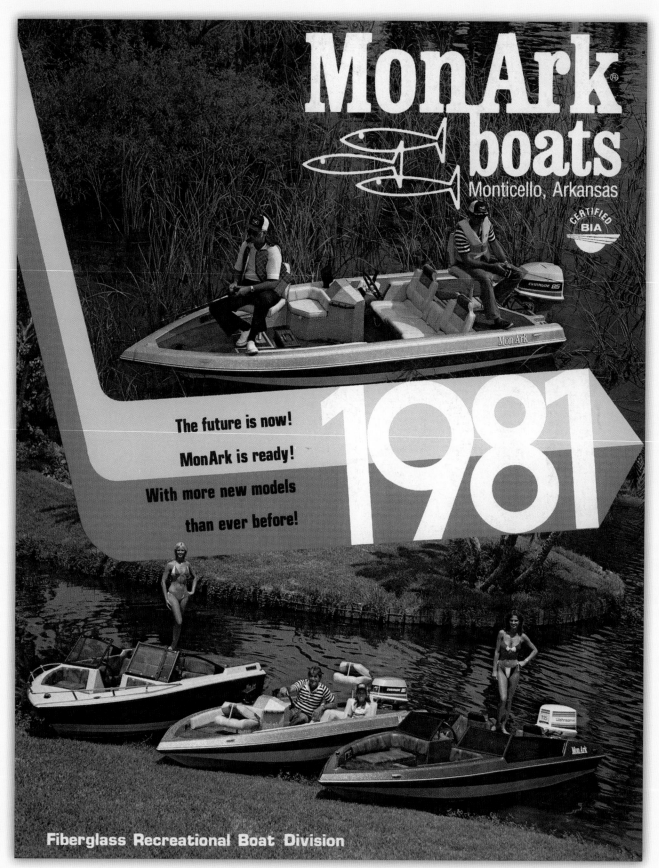

1981 MonArk catalog cover.

Chapter Four

A DECADE OF NEW CHALLENGES

s the 1980s began, MonArk continued in president Bob Lee's capable
hands while Zach McClendon found
himself busier than ever. He was president of Union
Bank, a responsibility that required daily attention and
energy. Sadly, Zach, Sr.'s health had begun to fail, leaving
Zach, Jr. to run Drew Foam, a company whose growth
had exceeded their initial expectations. In addition,
Zach had two new side businesses to tend: Engineering,
Manufacturing & Fabrication (E M & F) next door to
MonArk and Uniforce Electronics in Little Rock.

Almost since its inception, MonArk Workboat
Division's fortunes were tied to the oil industry in the Gulf
of Mexico, a trend that continued through the 1970s.
In the early 1980s, however, the Gulf oil market went
bust and the industry ground to a near halt. As a result,
MonArk's orders for crew boats and other boats related
to the oil industry were drastically reduced. To shore up
sales, the Workboat Division looked to government, law
enforcement, military, and municipal use boats.

MonArk started building fireboats in the early
1980s and production peaked in the mid-1990s. Cities
on the customer list for fireboats included Dallas,
Tampa, Toledo, Cincinnati, New York, Atlantic City,
New Orleans, Memphis, and Norfolk. Fireboat models were built to customer specifications and often
included fire and rescue equipment such as water-
pumping systems with up to 5,000 gallons per minute
at 150 pressure per square inch and sometimes specialized foam induction systems. Additional equipment
requested often included multiple monitors, independent diesel-driven fire pumps, rescue davits, and sirens,
hailers, and PA systems.

While intensifying their focus on the military market, MonArk began building boats designed for speed
and deeper waters. Some of the military contracts were
negotiated directly with foreign countries; others were
made through FMS (Foreign Military Sales), a purchasing arm of the U.S. Navy that purchased boats for
foreign countries where it was advantageous to U.S.
security, primarily in Central and South America at
that time. Negotiating these contracts included some
interesting travel experiences for MonArk's vice president, Don Law. On one occasion, he flew to Caracas,
Venezuela, and was transported to the country's interior
via a 30-foot boat carved out of a tree trunk with an
engine attached. MonArk's aluminum boats eventually
replaced some of those log canoes.

E M & F and Uniforce

The list of businesses that Zach McClendon has owned throughout his life is daunting and perfectly illustrates his appetite for business. Among them were World Wide Travel, a travel agency; Air Transportation, Inc., a charter air service; Drew Cotton Seed Oil Mill; farming operations; and Building Systems, a truss building operation. While some were not always stellar successes, as John points out, "Had Zach not created so many businesses—some of which were up while others were down—he might not have survived for fifty years on the boat business alone." Zach's creativity and energy gave him the ability to diversify and thereby protect his main company, MonArk Boats, through the tough times.

One of those businesses was Engineering, Manufacturing & Fabrication (E M & F), a machine shop that Zach started up around 1979 to internalize his supply chain for Drew Foam. E M & F specialized in foam manufacturing equipment and also did the machine work for MonArk and then SeaArk. It was dissolved around 1990.

At one time, MonArk bought their boat dashboards from a company in North Little Rock called Uniforce Electronics. According to Zach, they had hopes of building the digital gauge panels for automobile manufacturers. When that plan fell through, Zach bought the company for very little and they started making boat dash panels for marine manufacturers. Zach kept the company only for about seven years and in 1987 he sold it to High Voltage Electronics of Massachusetts. The company is still in business today in North Little Rock and is now owned by the man who operated it during Zach's ownership.

A promotional flyer created by MonArk in 1981 reported news of the (then) recent $1.5-million contract to the Haitian government for nine patrol boats and even featured a photo of Haitian sailors manning the .50-caliber machine guns on board. By 1981, the company was supplying military boats for countries located in the Caribbean, South America, Asia, Africa, and parts of Europe. The flyer also featured photos of two of MonArk's popular recreational products: a fiberglass ski boat and an aluminum bass boat, exemplifying the diversity of the company and its products.

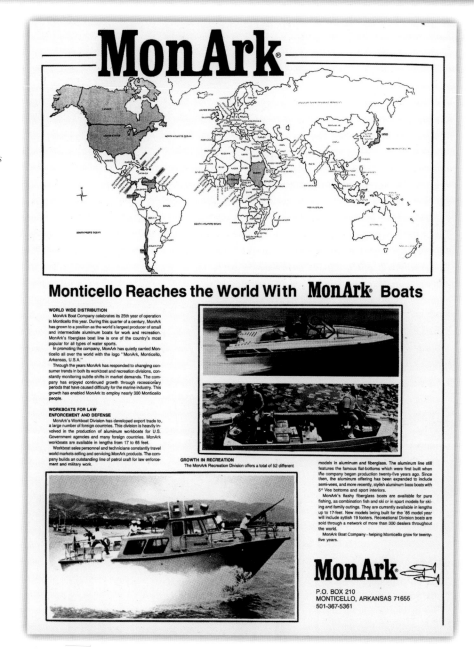

McClendon Dies Tuesday Night

Zach McClendon Sr., 75, of Monticello, owner and operator of Drew Foam Co. and founder of MonArk Boat Co., died Tuesday night at Drew Memorial Hospital following a lengthy illness.

A native of Strong (Union County), McClendon attended Arkansas College at Batesville, moving to Monticello in 1943 when he bought Drew Cotton Seed Oil Mill, of which he served as president since that time.

He was active in the Oil Seed Producers Association and served as director of the National Oil Producers Association and president of Valley Oil Seed Producers.

McClendon founded MonArk Boat Co. in 1959, along with his son, Zach Jr., and N.O. Judkins.

He served on the board of directors at Union Bank and Trust Co. for 34 years (1948-82) and was chairman the past 10 years. He was a member of the board of directors for Citizens Bank in Strong prior to coming to Drew County and was vice chairman of the Bank of West Memphis from 1972 through 1979.

McClendon was also a director for Ashley, Drew and Northern Railway.

He was a member of First Presbyterian Church, where he served as an elder and deacon.

Survivors include his wife, Pauline Johnson McClendon of Monticello; one son, Zach McClendon Jr. of Monticello; one daughter, Paddy Lee Estes of Washington, D.C.; two brothers, Bob McClendon of McGehee and Harold McClendon of Bastrop, La.; one sister, Blanche Hale of Bastrop, La.; two grandsons and two granddaughters.

Memorial services will be held at 3 p.m. tomorrow (Thursday) at First Presbyterian Church by Dr. Basil Hicks. Burial will be in Oakland Cemetery in Monticello by Stephenson Funeral Home.

The family requests that memorials be made to the building fund of First Presbyterian Church in Monticello.

ZACH MCCLENDON SR.
Dies At Age 75

Zach McClendon, Sr. died in 1982 at age seventy-five. Courtesy of the Advance Monticellonian.

In August 1981, MonArk built nine patrol boats, 40-foot diesel boats with twin engines, for a total of $1.5 million for Haiti. MonArk president Bob Lee was quoted in the *Commercial Appeal*, saying, "We're in the international market in a big way," citing sales to twenty-six foreign governments that included Nigeria, Panama, Japan, Vietnam, Saudi Arabia, Indonesia, Egypt, and England. The Haitian boats were to be used for patrol duty and drug interception. Three years prior, MonArk became an approved supplier of small commando boats for all NATO countries with a modified version of its standard 14-foot model. "The initial NATO approval was through the Dutch Army, which acquired 175 commando boats under their initial purchase," Lee said.

A Time to Mourn

In October 1982, Zach McClendon, Sr. passed away at the age of seventy-five following a long battle with a brain tumor. By the time of his death, Zach, Sr. had a long list of business and organizational achievements to his credit on top of his ownership in MonArk Boat Company and Drew Foam. Hearkening back to his earliest business venture, he was active in the Oil Seed Producers Association and served as director of the National Oil Producers Association and president of Valley Oil Seed Producers. He served on the Board of Directors of Union Bank in Monticello for thirty-one years, from 1951 to 1982, and was chairman for ten years prior to his death, a post that Zach, Jr. filled upon his father's death. Zach, Sr. was a member of the Board of Directors for Citizens Bank in Strong prior to moving to Drew County and was vice chairman of the Bank of West Memphis from 1972 through 1979. He was also a director for Ashley, Drew and Northern Railway. He was both an elder and a deacon of the First Presbyterian Church of Monticello. In short, he was a proverbial "pillar of the community."

Zach, Jr. is not a man given to visible signs of sentimentality, but to this day a veil of sadness comes over his face for just a moment when his father is mentioned. When asked if Zach himself imagined the success that MonArk might someday see, his primary thought is for his father. "I wish my dad was around to see the sophistication of the product that we are building today," he said. "I think he would have been in awe to see that." Sons want their fathers to be proud of them; a truism that is not altered by either time or age.

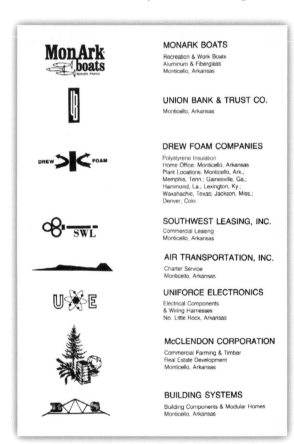

Zach's business card when he was at the height of his business holdings.

Miss USA

Throughout their history, the McClendon Companies have been a marketing and promotional machine. Don Law, vice president of marketing from the mid-1970s to mid-1980s, was capable of pulling off marketing feats worthy of much bigger companies.

Through Don's extensive network of contacts, he was able to use the Cypress Gardens facility located in Winter Park, Florida, including their photo boats and photo processing facilities, for many years to produce the first-class photography used at the time. The MonArk team shipped each year's new models to Florida on trucks around the first of June. The photo shoot usually took a week, and with some long hours and a little luck, the promotional material was ready in time for the summer dealer show.

On one trip to Florida, Don met Ron Rice, who was the founder and owner of Hawaiian Tropic sun tanning products. Rice had started his company making sun tan lotion in a bathtub and selling it himself one bottle at a time. Hawaiian Tropic was the leader in the market by the 1980s and Rice also happened to be a major sponsor and stakeholder in the Miss USA Pageant.

When Don met Ron in Florida, he saw a "marketing marriage made in Heaven." From 1980 to 1982, MonArk sponsored the Miss USA event. The winning contestant received a fiberglass MonArk S-1 runabout, which was a 16-foot inboard/ outboard-powered ski boat and one of the company's best sellers. In return, Miss USA would be on hand in the MonArk booth during the Dallas and Chicago trade shows as well as select dealer shows and promotions.

Don recalled that the exposure from this promotion was fantastic. "The winner of Miss USA went on to compete in the Miss Universe Pageant. That competition was televised with an audience of almost 700 million people in sixty-four countries, a tremendous advantage to MonArk and all the MonArk's dealers. Those girls were true celebrities and perfect matches for a fast, sexy-looking boat."

Don was the Arkansas regional director of the pageant in 1982. Always looking to add interest and excitement to whatever he did, the Miss USA Pageant was no exception that year. Don had been given an abaya, the traditional Middle Eastern garb for men, by a customer from Saudi Arabia several years prior. He asked a MonArk employee who worked in the engineering department (and had a dark complexion and dark mustache) to wear the clothing the night of the pageant. Don then hired a black Mercedes limousine and had the limo drop the "sheik" off at the pageant. Don had quietly started a rumor that a big oil tycoon from Saudi would be arriving at the pageant to meet Miss USA after she was crowned. The MonArk employee arrived and was escorted to the front row. Everyone was whispering and the "sheik" said nothing. After the pageant, the "sheik" was introduced to the newly crowned Miss USA and quickly exited to this limo and was whisked away, leaving a flurry of talk behind him. No one knew that Monday morning the "sheik" was back at work in the engineering department at MonArk!

MonArk Recreational Division manufacturer's representative *Gene Klund gets a stern look from Miss USA Jineane Ford during the MonArk Dealer Show in Hot Springs in 1981. Photo courtesy of the* Advance Monticellonian.

Miss USAs were used on MonArk's advertising after *Don Law established a sponsorship arrangement with the Miss USA Pageant.*

TERRI UTLEY
MISS USA 1982

U. S. A. finals to the Miss Hawaiian Tropic International Beauty Pageant / Beach Party held at Daytona Beach . . . Top four contestants win a trip to Hawaii to be TELECAST LIVE from Hawaii with Hawaiian tropic gift to the most beautiful to be a Porsche automobile and MonArk S-1 Sport Boat.

The over 100 U.S.A Daytona contestants represented more than 4,000 entrants from 62 regional contests whose promotions included Porsche & MonArk in advertising. Similar events are being held in more than 50 countries. More than 2,000 distributors, rep's and just plain workers around the world are involved in this Global search.

A key point to the MonArk dealer organization is that the conclusion will be telecast from Hawaii live in the height of the boat season with MonArk's S-1 and Porsche cars selected as Hawaiian Tropic's gift to the winner.

A 1982 news release issued by MonArk promoting the Miss USA Pageant sponsored by Hawaiian Tropic.

Good Times for Recreational Boats

Even though the economy was still officially in recession, the recreational boat division was doing well. In 1982, MonArk announced that they would begin manufacturing heavy-duty jon boats for commercial fishermen. The all-welded boats in 14-foot through 20-foot lengths were made of heavy-duty marine aluminum. Today, the majority of SeaArk Boats's recreational products are made of 0.125-gauge aluminum, giving them the advantage over competitors' products made with thinner stock.

MonArk's September 1983 newsletter announced that the dealers who attended their July show in Hot Springs, Arkansas, ordered 54 percent more products than the previous year, setting a new corporate record for the number of aluminum units sold. At the September Dallas show, dealers' orders more than doubled those of the previous year.

The 1980s would later be dubbed the "Me!Me!Me!" Decade. Baby boomers reached their prime income-earning years, and writer Tom Wolfe dubbed them the "splurge generation," making the mid-1980s a great time to be in the recreational boat business, particularly if you were selling a boat named "The McFast."

MonArk's 1984 catalog published the results of a test evaluation conducted by *Powerboat Magazine* on MonArk's McFast VSF-16 and S-1 outboards at Cypress Gardens, Florida. The reviews were overwhelming. Readers had this to say about the S-1:

"You have to wonder what more you could want from a runabout smaller than 17 feet."

"The S-1 is among the finest sub-17-footers that I've ever driven."

"The S-1 needed only slightly more than two seconds to get on plane. Incredible."

The reviews were equally enthusiastic for the McFast VSF-16:

"The MonArk McFast VSF-16 is a tremendous step forward in bass boat development."

"The most impressive surprise was its ability to handle rough water. The boat's marvelously solid construction left us with a very soft and dry ride."

Workboats

Bruce Neimeth was named president of MonArk in October 1983 when Bob Lee left the company for his own entrepreneurial pursuits. Johnny Smith was made sales manager of the Workboat Division in 1984 and was given responsibility for developing MonArk's military business through GSA (General Services Administration) contracts. "If you could get a boat on GSA contract," Johnny said, "you didn't have to compete or bid it. You could sell it direct to them by contract." The slump in the oil workboat business continued, and the military contracts became increasingly important to MonArk.

In 1983, MonArk designed the Barracuda 27 as a unique new anti-drug smuggling patrol boat. Designed for use primarily in the Gulf Coast area, the boat closely resembled those used by the drug smugglers themselves. MonArk's engineering team worked with law enforcement agents to design a

A MonArk Fiberglass S1 in the mid-1980s. The company became a leading producer of fish and ski products during the 1970s and 1980s.

During the height of the Gulf of Mexico oil boom in the late 1970s and early 1980s, the MonArk Workboat Division focused on crew boat production.

A staple product for MonArk workboats in the 1970s and 1980s, a 40-foot crew boat, plies the lower Mississippi River.

In 1983, MonArk delivered eight oil spill vessels to the U.S. Navy Supervisor of Salvage. The aluminum boats were a new class of vessels used principally for towing oil spill booms with skimmers and as working platforms for salvage and clean-up. The 24-foot boats were designed to assist with emergency containment and had removable bow sections to allow shipment of two boats together on a C130 aircraft.

Zach McClendon, Jr., Governor Bill Clinton, Bruce Neimeth, and Henry Mariani at the press conference where MonArk announced its expansion as a result of the contract to build thirty-seven military boats for Venezuela, 1984. Photo courtesy of the Advance Monticellonian.

boat that could withstand the rigors of offshore patrol work day-in and day-out. The Barracuda was an all-welded boat with a deep-vee hull design, enabling the boat to fall on plane in five seconds from a dead stop and achieve maximum speeds of approximately sixty miles per hour. Its speed and maneuvering capability made it an ideal surprise and pursuit vehicle.

The year 1983 turned out to be a banner year for the Workboat Division at MonArk. The U.S. Navy purchased nine 35-foot workboats for salvage work, the U.S. Army Corps of Engineers purchased a 40-foot buoy-tending barge for work in Savannah, Georgia, and the Chicago Police Department, which had already purchased two 32-foot patrol boats, signed a contract for a 42-foot patrol boat for service on Lake Michigan. The state of Florida purchased several steel hull Hydrilla Removers, shallow draft vessels with a steel hull shaped like a towboat for clearing hydrilla from waterways. These larger boats were just a sample of the highly diverse and profitable product line that the MonArk Workboat Division had developed over the previous twenty years.

The Venezuelan Expansion

In January 1984, MonArk made the front page of the *Advance Monticellonian* as they announced a major expansion in its workboat production facilities and their selection for a $4-million-plus contract with Venezuela for thirty-seven military boats.

Arkansas Governor Bill Clinton was on hand for the announcement at the Capitol Hotel in Little Rock. He congratulated MonArk, saying, "At a time when the economy of Southeast Arkansas is depressed, when lately so many of the announcements have been about closing of plants, this comes as exciting news."

Bruce Neimeth said that the Venezuelan contract meant the hiring of approximately eighty additional

A Magnetic Personality

Zach McClendon has an undeniably magnetic personality. While that may sound like a compliment—and most of the time it is— it is also not without its pitfalls. After all, a magnet that's aimed indiscriminately can attract a lot of scrap metal. In truth, over the years Zach has managed to attract some rather colorful people throughout his life; people who also "march to the tune of a different drummer." John's theory is that Zach "wants to believe the pitch" and thus falls victim to people who, without any real substance, are able to make a good "pitch." Then, as John says, they "roll down the highway together until the money runs out." Listening to his son's analysis, Zach just smiles the kind of smile that says, "I know you're right but what can I tell you?" and calls it his "contribution to the redistribution of wealth."

In addition to Zach's interesting array of potential business partners, MonArk had its share of colorful employees. One such fellow, let's just call him "Charles," was known for his tall tales. For instance, one time he was testing a boat on the Arkansas River and ran it aground. It wasn't an unforgivable offense; just one of those things that sometimes happens. What was so preposterous was that his explanation as to how he got the boat out was that he called the Corps of Engineers and had them open the floodgates to raise the river two feet!

This fellow was also known for making wild promises to women he met at the boat shows by claiming he was the owner of the company. In the late 1970s, Dick Dickinson took a call one Friday afternoon from a young lady, asking to speak to "Charles McClendon." Confused, Dick asked for more specifics from the young lady who explained that she'd met the son of the owner of MonArk at a boat show the previous week and having had a good time together, they parted company with the understanding that she was to be at the airport the following Friday to meet the company airplane he would send to pick her up. She was at the airport, awaiting a plane that hadn't arrived, and was mighty disappointed to learn that the owner's son was only ten years old.

Sometimes, though, these eccentric personalities worked in MonArk's favor.

For instance, there was the time MonArk delivered a 42-foot boat they'd made for a crew boat leasing company. Bob Lee, who was president of MonArk at the time, got a call from someone telling him the company was in receivership. Knowing that meant they'd never get paid, Bob contacted the fellow and said, "I don't care what it takes—go get that boat." The fellow drove a truck in the middle of the night down to South Louisiana and used a pair of bolt cutters to cut the locks the bank had put on the gate, somehow managed to get the boat loaded, and brought it back. He got within twenty miles of Monticello when a policeman stopped him, questioning the logic of an oversized load going down the highway in the middle of the night. The fellow simply explained that he was repossessing a boat from a bankrupt owner, to which the cop simply said, "Okay, see ya." Most people would have been shaking in their boots but this guy slipped away like Houdini squirming out of a strait jacket.

Though this fellow's job was test engineer for MonArk, in truth he was the guy they sent to do the things no one else wanted to do. Like the time MonArk delivered a crew boat to Houston that, for reasons unknown, the Coast Guard refused to certify. He was sent down to face the customer who told him that unless they could get the boat certified very soon, they would refuse to accept delivery and demand their money back. His instructions from the MonArk side were clear: "Get the boat accepted—we don't care what it takes." Getting all kinds of excuses from the Coast Guard inspector as to why he couldn't get to the boat, the fellow hired a helicopter to the tune of $600 per hour to go get the inspector, wait for him to inspect the boat, sign off on it, and then fly him back to his post. After all, there was a $300,000 boat on the line! Sometimes when a guy is that crazy, you really do want him on your side.

A MonArk workboat model 2810-V on patrol in service for the U.S. Coast Guard, 1985.

people, an increase of 33 percent in its work force, equating to an additional $405,000 in annual payroll.

MonArk's new 7,200-square-foot building addition at the plant, located at the old Drew Oil Mill site, was used for the construction of the Venezuelan boats. "This is the largest contract ever received by MonArk Boat Company," Neimeth said, "and it is representative of the growth the company began experiencing in 1983. Our sales increased nearly 22 percent last year and we are currently negotiating and finalizing contracts for several more large transactions." The contract with Venezuela included twelve 42-foot gunboats, ten 21-foot utility patrol vessels, and fifteen 16-foot military escort boats. MonArk was chosen for the contract because of their ability to satisfy all of the government's needs in one company, making MonArk unique among boat builders in the world.

Some of MonArk's military contract business began with the Coast Guard. Johnny Smith recalled, "We were bidding on 'TanB's,' Trailer-able Aids to Navigation Boats. We got contracts to build those boats and developed a relationship with the Coast Guard." That eventually led to contracts with the Navy, initially building oil spill control boats.

While the government contracts proved to be good for MonArk, they came with exacting sets of specifications and stringent inspections, forcing the improvements in quality control that had been a challenge for MonArk. The boats were taken to Pine Bluff for testing on the Arkansas River. Quality assurance specialists at the time, Kim Coon and Audie Curtis, put the boats through their courses to insure that the boats performed to the customer's expectations. Before putting the boat in the water, dockside tests were run to check the electrical systems. Flaws as small as a half-inch scratch on the windshield were enough to send the boat back for replacement parts. Once in the water, an incline protractor was used to measure the angle at which the front of the boat stuck out of the water at different speeds. They also noted the speed at which the boat "breaks plane," that is, when the front end dips back down after rising during acceleration. Turning radius was measured, a decibel meter was used to measure the loudness of the engine, and the tachometer was checked against a calibrator connected to the engine.

In January 1985, MonArk began work on a contract with the Naval Sea System Command to build multiple 26-foot fiberglass personnel carriers at an estimated cost of $5 million. The boats, which were carried on United States destroyers and cruisers all over the world, were used to ferry personnel, mail, and cargo from ship to shore when the big ships were in harbor. Up to this point, MonArk's fiberglass production had been strictly in recreational products and they soon found they were unprepared for the challenges involved in building fiberglass products to extreme military specifications. Nonetheless, the decision had been made to take on the project in an effort to explore an entirely new market. The project was financially unsuccessful, but it illustrates Zach's fearlessness, borne out of his confidence in his own abilities and that of his employees. Despite the financial ramifications, MonArk completed their obligations under the contract, displaying a rare level of integrity and commitment to customer satisfaction.

In September 1986, Charles Mann was named president of MonArk. By that time, MonArk's reputation for specialty boat-building had spread far and wide. That's why, when the U.S. Air Force and Navy needed a boat for training pilots who might find themselves bailing out of a plane into the sea, they contacted MonArk. The 42-foot U.S. Air Force Parasail Training Craft was designed to lift survival trainees suspended from a canopy as high as 400 feet into the air, at which point they could release a towline and parachute into the water. Naval Sea Systems Command contracted with MonArk for nine such boats for use at the Air Force Survival School.

Charles W. Mann was president of MonArk just prior to the sale to Brunswick in 1988.

A 41-foot U.S. Air Force parasail training craft built by MonArk in 1986.

A MonArk Fiberglass VSF16, one of many models the company built in the early 1980s.

At the same time, MonArk built a 30-foot all-aluminum transportation barge for the Panama Canal Commission's use in their survey operation. Johnny Smith, who was national sales manager for MonArk at the time, was quoted as saying, "These rugged barges typify MonArk's twenty-seven-year reputation for its ability to consistently meet the challenge of rigorous standards for a brutal environment."

The Fiberglass Dilemma

Coming off a seven-year sales streak, by 1987 the recreational boat business found itself staring at yet another economic downturn.

MonArk's fiberglass boat line was particularly suffering from the recession, a situation that was made even worse by the glut of manufacturers that rushed to enter a market known for its relatively easy start-up. Though very popular, fiberglass was not always a profitable product and is one of the few decisions Zach McClendon questions in hindsight regardless of how logical a decision it was at the time. "It was a new material (in 1960) and it was catching on like wildfire. It was easy to get into and didn't take much capital," Zach recalled. It's easy to see how Zach's creative mind was tempted by the design possibilities associated with fiberglass products. "With aluminum you can make straight lines, more or less. If you have a mold, you can make fiberglass look like a spaceship." Regardless of their eco-

nomic viability, MonArk's fiberglass products contributed greatly to building MonArk's name recognition and reputation, and opened avenues of growth that might not otherwise have materialized. MonArk exited the fiberglass boat business around 1987.

The End of the MonArk Era

The boat manufacturers weren't the only ones feeling the effects of the economy. Two of the big motor manufacturers, OMC and Brunswick, were looking for new distribution vehicles for selling motors and according to Dick Dickinson, "They started gobbling up little independent boat businesses over a period of several years."

Brunswick approached Zach about the possibility of purchasing MonArk's recreational boat business. Some of life's travails can only be truly appreciated by those who experience them firsthand. Selling a business that one has built from the ground up and nurtured over decades is one of them. Considering the time, energy, and money that Zach invested in MonArk over the years, combined with an uncommon sense of obligation he felt to the employees who'd helped him build the company, one can only imagine how difficult a decision this must have been for him. Feeling his back was to the wall, in April 1988, Zach agreed to sell both the recreational boat business and the MonArk name to Brunswick. Putting the best possible light on a heart-

SeaArk Marine engineering manager and talented artist Ronnie McGehee created many humorous comic covers parodying people and events within the company. This particular drawing from April 1988 depicts the anxiety over the sale of the MonArk Recreational Division. Drawing courtesy of Ronnie McGehee.

along with the inland location of the plant. Robert Trammel, a certified public accountant from Little Rock, was named president of SeaArk Marine in January 1988. Longtime employee Willie Brennon was promoted to vice president of manufacturing and Johnny Smith was named vice president of sales and marketing.

However difficult a decision it must have been, the sale to Brunswick was, in some ways, a blessing in disguise. It provided SeaArk the resources needed to invest in upgrading their production facility and gave them a renewed focus on the design and marketing of workboats. As part of the announcement, Zach was quoted saying, "We will continue to sell and manufacture high-quality mid-range workboats from 20 to 60 feet in length to our commercial, government, and industrial customers throughout the world."

rending decision, Zach was quoted in the *Arkansas Democrat*, saying, "We felt like it was the right time to sell that part of the business. Now we can concentrate on commercial vessels."

As part of the deal with Brunswick, Zach agreed to provide his input under a consulting agreement for a specific time period but, quickly frustrated with the politics of a large corporation, the arrangement didn't last long. As Robin observed, "Always a 'tell-it-like-it-is' sort of guy, Zach was as eager to stop attending the meetings as they probably were to have him stop coming!"

SeaArk Marine

The remaining MonArk Workboat Division was renamed SeaArk Marine, Inc. Employee Gay Rabb Griffith came up with the name as an homage to the original MonArk name (the word "SeaArk" could stand for Southeast Arkansas). It also represented "Sea" as in ocean, and "Ark" as in Arkansas, combining the saltwater environment to which most of the boats were shipped

MonArk's Workboat Division was renamed SeaArk Marine. Zach is pictured here after the sale of the MonArk name and Recreational Division to Brunswick.

MonArk Workboat Division police boats (foreground) built for the city of Chicago patrol Lake Michigan with the famous skyline in the background.

At the time of the sale to Brunswick, MonArk's boats were in use in all fifty states and numerous countries. The company's client list included governmental departments and agencies in twenty-five different countries, most of the major oil companies, a wide range of industrial concerns, and even Walt Disney World.

In 1989, the newly named SeaArk Marine snagged a $4-million contract to build ten gunboats for the tiny country of El Salvador for coastal patrol, boundary protection, and drug interdiction. According to Johnny Smith, they began negotiations with El Salvador as early as 1983, but the funding, provided through the U.S. government's Military Assistance Program, didn't become available until 1988. El Salvador chose SeaArk on the merits of the twelve similar boats the company built for Venezuela. MonArk's Workboat Division's reputation for quality and service enjoyed continued recognition under its new name, SeaArk Marine, Inc.

In 1990, the U.S. Marine Corps and Navy cooperated in a study to evaluate the future of riverine or "brown water" warfare. The first such study since 1964, it was conducted as part of the Atlantic Fleet's "Solid Shield" exercise to determine deficiencies in riverine capabilities. Chosen primarily because of their ability to meet an urgent deadline, SeaArk Marine, Inc. built seven 35-foot "Stinger" riverine assault craft in less than ninety days.

Brunswick Closes the Monticello Plant

In January 1990, Brunswick announced the closing of the Monticello plant. Citing the continued softness in the recreational marine market, the company moved the production of the aluminum boat models to other Brunswick fishing boat plants. Aware of the current market conditions, Zach was not critical of the decision but his compassion went out to the employees who were impacted by it. "I am really disappointed and feel for these people," Zach was quoted as saying in the January 10, 1990 issue of *The Advance Monticellonian*. "There are a lot of longterm people at that plant—some have been there since MonArk's inception." Not one to express idle sympathies, Zach saw to it that SeaArk absorbed as many laid-off employees as possible.

In the years that followed the sale to Brunswick, Zach became aware that the MonArk name carried even more value than he'd previously thought. To this day, the company still gets letters and calls for MonArk, a name that remains known worldwide. Had he known the true value of the MonArk name, greater negotiating power might have been brought to bear on the Brunswick buyers. Regardless, the name MonArk lives on to this day, synonymous with the man who built it with his own two hands. That's something no one can take away.

Source:

The *Commercial Appeal*, August 2, 1981.

TEAMWORK

Many Dedicated and Talented Individuals
Create the Teams that Make the MonArk/SeaArk Story a Success!

The management, engineering, and administrative teams for MonArk Workboat Division during the mid-1980s included (left to right), front row: Billy Taylor, Gerald Bates, unknown, Karen Cook, Nick Florentine, and Ronnie McGehee; middle row: Ronnie Woodall, Jim Vance, Lester Halbert, E. G. Dendy, Ricky Pierce, and Richard Ortego; back row: John King, Virgil Grant, Jim Barron, Jerry Smith, and Kim Coon.

The MonArk Recreational Division team, circa 1983.

The MonArk workboat team, circa 1985.

The SeaArk Marine production crew poses for a Christmas card on a 48-foot crew boat, 1989.

The SeaArk Marine team poses for a photo in front of six 35-foot Riverine Assault Craft built for the U.S. Marine Corps in 1990.

SeaArk Marine sales team, circa 1995. Left to right: John McClendon, Pete Peterson, Ken McFalls, Rixby Trahan, Fred Rode, Paul Hureau, Bob Neelon, Rob MacMahon, and Jerry Smith.

The SeaArk Boats team poses outside SeaArk Marine in 1996 shortly before their move back to the old MonArk plant on Patton Street.

The SeaArk Marine team in front of two recently completed 40-foot Dauntless patrol boats in 1997.

*The SeaArk Marine team with a sampling
of the wide variety of products offered
by the company around 1998.*

*Left to right: Bob
Neelon, Jerry Smith,
Ken McFalls, and
Lester Halbert in
front of a 44-foot
SeaArk Marine
Dauntless bound for
service in Peru, 2000.*

The "cream of the crop" SeaArk Boats team, following the company's scale-back in 2002.

The SeaArk Marine team poses for a picture after a ceremony and moment of silence on September 11, 2002 to remember the 9/11 tragedy. The city of Monticello held the event on the town square and SeaArk Marine displayed several boats sold to agencies for use in combating terrorism.

MERRY CHRISTMAS
& HAPPY NEW YEAR
Best Wishes
The SeaArk Boats Team
Christmas 2005

The SeaArk Boats team poses for a Christmas card in 2005.

The Camp.

Chapter Five

THE McCLENDON FAMILY CAMP

Though Zach and his family have called the city of Monticello home since 1943, the collective McClendon family heart belongs to an area that extends from the Saline River on the west to the lowlands of the Mississippi Delta on the east.

Hunting, fishing, and camping is like breathing to most young boys in southern Arkansas, and when a friend's father introduced Zach to the world of the outdoors, what was at first recreation grew into a legendary passion for the sport and a deep love and appreciation for flora and fauna of all varieties.

Zach was consumed with hunting, fishing, taxidermy, woodcraft, and all things natural. The Trotter Brake area east of Monticello was a favorite hunting ground, and Robin will tell you that the attic of her grandmother's house, in which she now lives, is also home to many of the animals on which Zach practiced his taxidermy skills and preserved un-hatched birds, snakes, and frogs in bottles. Robin refers to her attic as "Zach's personal Museum of Natural History" and recalls hearing her grandmother Pauline tell the story of the day she came home to find a sign in the yard and people trooping through the house to the attic to see the museum. As Robin said, "Zach was, of course, charging admission!"

Zach also spent a lot of time with friends on the Saline River, which was where some of his earliest boat-building experiences took place. Rising out of the Ouachita Mountains, the Saline is a tributary of the Little River and part of the Mississippi River watershed. Zach passed his love for the Saline River on to his daughter, Robin, who grew to appreciate and love the river as much as Zach does and now has a place of her own along its banks. "I think our family has an unusual appreciation for nature and the outdoors," Robin said, "and that certainly came through Zach and our mother. I love the outdoors—we all do."

As a young man, Zach dreamed of buying up the land in the Delta in order to protect and preserve its pristine nature. During the early 1960s, Zach, Sr., Zach, Jr., and business partner Hamp Pugh purchased some cotton ground bordering the Trotter Brake area. At that time, Zach, Sr. still had ownership in several South Arkansas cotton gins. Near that area was several hundred acres of old-growth hardwood forest; the Ables Creek Watershed and another cypress slough named Mink Track Brake. Zach, Jr. saw the opportunity to create a hunting and fishing paradise. With his father's help, Zach eventually acquired 3,500 acres in the area, one parcel at a time.

The property is a combination of row crop farmland, recreational woods, and water located between the Selma and Tillar communities in the Delta region of Eastern Drew County, Arkansas. A dilapidated old government barn stood abandoned and neglected in the center of the property. Robin remembers going with Zach to see the property, Zach with the omnipresent yellow pad and black felt-tip pen he used to make notes and sketches as he and Robin walked through the old barn.

In 1967, Zach gutted the rustic structure and made a camp house lodge out of it. Dubbed the "Mink Track Hunting Club," it had only one bathroom and nothing in the way of modern conveniences. Besides being a recreational haven, the Camp is still part of a working agricultural farm.

John McClendon, who shares Zach's passion for hunting, has a tremendous appreciation for his father's conservation efforts. "Zach carefully crafted a hunting and fishing paradise on the acreage," he said. "He dredged canals, planted thousands of trees, and built reservoirs, dams, and bridges, along with hundreds of deer stands and dozens of duck blinds. Always with an eye to improving wildlife habitat and outdoor opportunities, he has invested his time, energy, and money into long-range rewards, knowing that many of these will come to fruition long after he is gone."

The Camp Burns

In December 1977, two fellows broke into the hunting club at the Camp and burglarized the place. After celebrating perhaps a bit too much, they returned to the Camp a few hours later and set it ablaze, presumably in an attempt to cover up the crime. It burned to the ground.

What the McClendons consider paradise—the Trotter Brake at their Mink Track Camp in the Delta. The area provides them with fishing, various game hunting, and a place to relax with family and friends.

Though he was only nine years old, John's memory of the pile of ashes is very vivid. "There was a chimney standing and a tin roof on the ground. There was nothing left—the old cypress was just like a tinderbox." Robin also remembers that night—"one of only two times I have seen Zach cry." The thieves kept some of the guns and threw others in the swamp as they retreated. They were eventually caught, albeit for other crimes, and sentenced to prison. Refusing to let them get the upper hand, Zach rebuilt the entire place to resemble the original government barn's exterior. He added extra bedrooms, bathrooms, and a tack room, plus some modern conveniences such as central heat and air conditioning—and complete security systems inside and out.

In typical Zach McClendon style, an 1850s-era log cabin was added to the Camp in 1994. Sitting on a nearby property, it was scheduled for demolition to make room for new development. When he went with his father to take a look at it, John felt sure Zach was going to tell the owner it was too dilapidated and that he didn't want it. "It was completely overgrown with briars and honeysuckle vines," John said, and to make matters worse, one of the rooms had been gutted by fire years ago. However, the next thing John knew, Zach was on the phone with the house-movers asking how fast they could move it to the Camp. The restored cypress log home provides respite for Zach and his guests with a broad front porch perfect for watching the sun set behind the cotton fields.

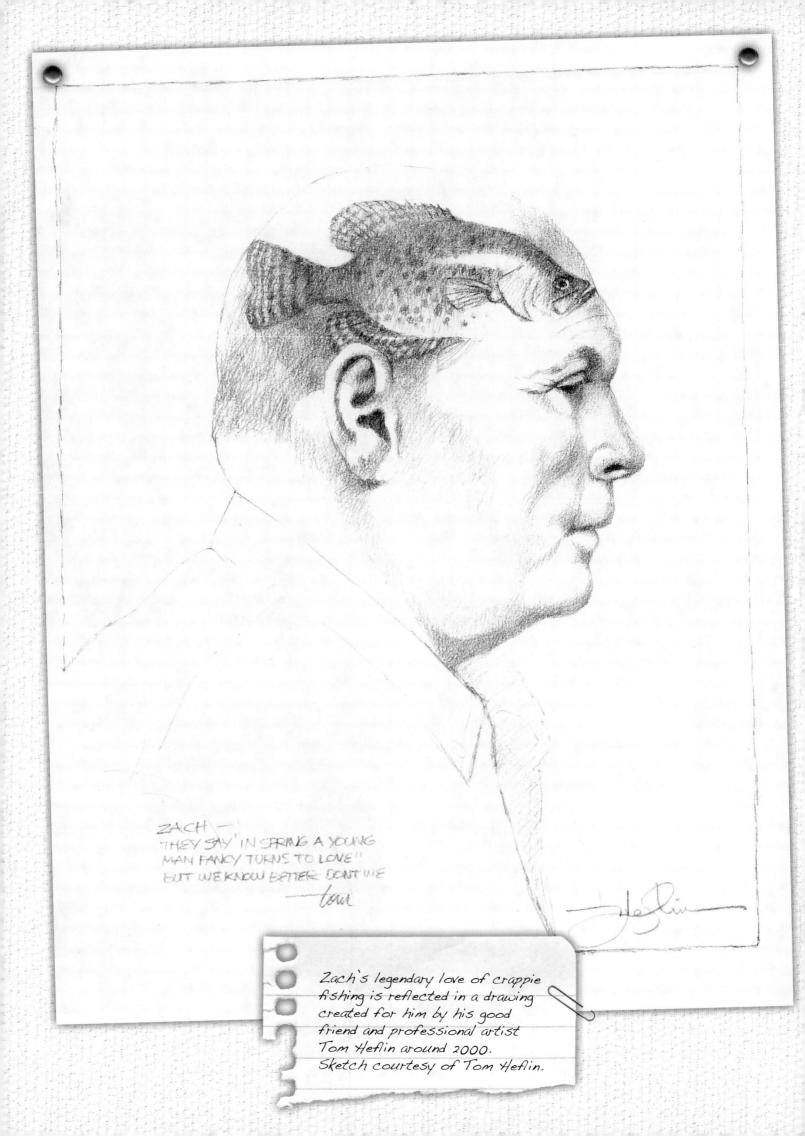

Zach's legendary love of crappie fishing is reflected in a drawing created for him by his good friend and professional artist Tom Heflin around 2000.
Sketch courtesy of Tom Heflin.

Not only has the Camp provided Zach with an opportunity to indulge his passion for conservation, it was also the perfect place for unleashing his extraordinary creativity. As Robin said, "I think Zach is about half architect and designer. Every project he gets involved with is really exceptional! He easily looks at an old barn and sees a comfortable camp house. He took that old cabin with the dogtrot and made an ideal little retreat for himself. He has this ability to see what is not there and then find a way to make it what he wants. Not many people have vision like that."

Robin recruited Zach's creativity when she purchased her own cabin on the Saline River. Since the river is prone to flooding, all the camps are built up on stilts. Zach suggested she put a deck on her cabin, even though the slope at the river's edge meant that the deck would be thirty feet off of the ground. Numerous tall trees, which neither Zach nor Robin would ever consider cutting down, also complicated the project. Zach, on the other hand, was simply inspired by those challenges. As Robin describes it, "He designed it, figured it out, had it winding through the trees, and had telephone poles from his "stash" (because he never gets rid of anything) put into the ground. The deck is what makes my cabin a wonderful and relaxing place to hang out. He also designed a floating dock on which I keep my boat so no matter what level the river is at, the dock floats and the boat can be accessed. Both projects were well beyond my capacity to envision and both turned out great."

Family Tales

No matter how many stories you listen to of life at the Camp, you still only get a glimpse of what this place means to the McClendon family. Both Robin and John speak of this place with joy at all the memories its name invokes and with reverence for a place that has held the heart and soul of the McClendon family throughout their lifetimes. "There's really no other place quite like it in the world," says John McClendon, who literally grew up hunting and fishing the property. "You can go to a hundred other private or commercial hunting clubs and won't find the authentic, rustic personality of this place or the diversity of wildlife it offers. We have had so many good times at the Camp with our family and friends; you just start to feel happy when you turn down the road headed down there."

Parents often give their children lessons in ways they don't even realize. For instance, Robin remembers the time that she and Zach were at the Camp by themselves when she was just eight or nine years old. She was building a fort out of some leftover tin when she took a bad fall. The piece of tin she was holding cut a gash in her upper arm. She recalled, "It was bleeding pretty good and I went inside to show Zach. He wiped it off and sprayed some Foil burn spray on it. It was the only first-aid remedy we had down there. He told me I would be fine and I believed him." Though Robin's mother was upset over the cut that should have been stitched, and Robin herself carries the physical scar, what she also carries is the clear message that prepared her for the challenges that life brings—when

Zach passed on his love of the outdoors to John. Here, they're pictured with their "catch of the day," ducks and catfish.

Left to right: Ralph Chastain, Jake Taylor, John Bailey, MonArk President Bob Lee, Jim Vance, Carl Franz, and E. G. Dendy pose for a photo during one of the many company dinners held at Zach's Camp, circa late 1970s.

alligators were released. John was only four years old at the time, but the event made quite an impression on him.

"My father and I went to a cypress brake near the camp and met a man in a flatbed pickup with a large white box on the back. He opened the box and gingerly slipped out a bound and tied six-foot alligator. All of the alligators were 'hog-tied' and had large rubber bands around their snouts. The idea was to untie the four feet and then use a long pole with a blunt hook to remove the snout bands from a distance and allow the gator to scamper away into his new home.

"The procedure worked perfectly until the sixth or seventh alligator was slid out of the box. When this particular gator's feet were freed and it was time to snatch the rubber bands off from a distance, the hook slipped out somehow and the gator was poised to get away with the rubber bands on his nose still in place.

"Even though it happened years ago, I can see it like it was yesterday. My dad leaped onto the back of the alligator and attempted to pin him to the ground before he got away with his nose still bound and no way to eat. The melee that ensued was something between a WWF Championship match and a greased pig race. The gator was thrashing, my dad was cussing, and the biologist was frantically trying to get the pole hook back

adversity hits, pick yourself up, brush yourself off, and get back in the game.

In typical older-sibling fashion, Robin also remembers one time when John had a party at the Camp that included lots of frog-leg cooking plus the usual music and dancing.

When someone suggested they sprinkle cornmeal on the floor to make it more conducive to dancing, Eddie Flemister, Larry Flemister's son and John's longtime friend, reached for the dishwashing powder. According to Robin, "Everyone danced for hours." Apparently everyone was happy except the caretakers, who weren't too thrilled with what the ground-in dishwashing soap had done to the linoleum floors.

One of the events that looms largest in John's memory, however, has to do with the time when alligators, that "perfectly evolved and adapted amphibious icon of the natural southern wetlands" as he calls them, were reintroduced to Mink Track Brake.

In 1972, the Arkansas Game and Fish Commission contacted Zach and asked him to participate in their program to reintroduce alligators to the Delta region. Zach's fondness for animals of all sorts made it easy for him to agree and that summer a dozen or so

A young John McClendon and boyhood friend Anthony Brown duck hunting with Zach in a promotional photo, circa 1978.

The Great Arkansas Alligator Hunt

In 1972, the Arkansas Game and Fish Commission approached Zach about the possibility of releasing a dozen or so alligators into the wetlands of his property as part of a reintroduction program. Zach agreed and over the years, the alligators increased in number and were thriving in the Delta region of Eastern Drew County.

However, a few incidents occurred in recent years that indicated that the alligators were becoming perhaps a bit too comfortable in this setting. The chickens, goats, and other animals that resided in the farmyard near the cypress slough at the McClendons' Camp were becoming easy midnight snacks for the alligators as they became bolder and bolder. Even John's Labrador retriever, Juicy, narrowly escaped an alligator's jaws during one of her frequent dips in the canal to cool off from the summer heat. The Camp manager's pit bull terrier wasn't as lucky as Juicy, disappearing in a swirl of water. And the dozen or so cats that freely roamed the Camp property had recently dwindled to three.

One particularly large alligator had been cruising the cypress brake and canals near the Camp the entire summer of 2007. Whether or not he was the perpetrator of the aforementioned deeds, he certainly qualified as a "nuisance gator," so when the Arkansas Game and Fish Commission held the first legal alligator season in 2007, he became the target of the Great Arkansas Alligator Hunt. John McClendon tells the story:

"The plan was simple: the gator was lying near a dock and we would attempt to snare him, dispatch him, and then use a boat to get him to the bank. And that is exactly what happened—sort of.

"I started with the eighty-inch snare on a ten-foot pole and carefully started to slip it over the tip of his nose and back toward his neck. Not quite big enough to pass over the 560-pound alligator's fat jowls, the snare stopped somewhere short of the back of his jaw and the gator, now alert to something amiss, started to slip backward into the water.

"I yanked as hard as I could on the rope, freeing it from the pole, and held on for dear life. The snare closed up somewhere around mid-snout, but the snare itself was on the top of his snout, allowing a little too much jaw movement for comfort. With the alligator thrashing about, I passed the first line off to Patrick and we immediately got another snare on his snout."

The team, consisting of John, his father Zach, cousin Patrick Harris, and friend Anthony Brown, managed to lift the gator's head up with the second line, the first line having been wrapped around the dock and rendered useless.

"My dad agreed that I should take the shot while we had control of the alligator's head. I leveled the Remington 870 off about three feet from his head. I squeezed the trigger and the water erupted into a mosaic of white water, gator meat, and blood."

When finally hauled to shore, the alligator measured twelve feet, eight inches long and "tipped the scales at 560 pounds," giving the McClendon team bragging rights to the largest alligator harvested during Arkansas' first legal hunt.

Zach stands over the first-ever, and largest, legally harvested alligator in the state of Arkansas at the McClendon family Camp, September 2007.

Duck hunting on Trotter Brake. All the McClendons love the outdoors. The woods and waters here have entertained many customers over the years.

January 2002, John and Anthony were duck hunting with another friend, Tom Pat Heflin, near Bayou Bartholomew, which flows near the Camp. Ordinarily, gators would not be active in such cold temperatures, but a four-foot alligator wasn't playing by the rules that day and when Anthony stepped on what he thought was a log, the gator clamped onto Anthony's calf, refusing to let go. Anthony used the unloaded barrel of his twelve-gauge shotgun to pry open the gator's jaws and freed his leg while John grabbed it by the back of the neck.

Strictly Business?

John McClendon will be the first to tell you that in the McClendon clan, family and business go hand in hand. As a result, the Camp has seen many meetings and been the entertaining center for the myriad customers, dealers, and employees who have been part of the MonArk/SeaArk circle of friends.

In the late 1990s, Zach sent John and Doug Thornton to Nebraska to negotiate with Cabela's, the sports outfitting retailer, for the manufacture of a variety of aluminum fabricated accessories, mostly for waterfowl hunting. The product line only lasted for a couple of years, but when the original deal was in the works the crew from Cabela's, including their top three vice presidents, visited the Camp for some duck hunting and had such a good time they sent a second group down on the corporate jet the very next week. As John says, this was "one of many hunting ventures where the Camp helped secure business. People involved in the boating world generally like the outdoors and the Camp is a great tool for entertaining them."

under the rubber bands to pull them off. In the end, the rubber bands were finally removed and my dad and the gator hastily (and gladly) parted company."

The alligator had been gone from the wetlands of South Arkansas for nearly a century, the result of over-harvesting and loss of habitat. In 2002, the Arkansas Game and Fish Commission hired Tommy Hines, an alligator specialist formerly with the state of Florida, to conduct a survey around the McClendon property and other places in Arkansas. He declared the reintroduction a success, estimating hundreds of alligators on the McClendon property alone.

John took many a friend hunting or fishing at the Camp over the years and never tired of watching their faces as they laid eyes on one of the alligators. One time, John and hunting buddies Anthony Brown and Todd Henry were out frog hunting. Somehow they accidentally pinned an eight-foot gator under their 14-foot jon boat. On one side of the boat was a set of snapping jaws and on the other a wildly thrashing tail.

Another story even made the local newspapers. On a cold day in

Zach with his retriever, Chance, at the McClendon family Camp in 2005.

Another story that combines both business and the McClendons' brand of adventure has become legendary in SeaArk lore. It involves a man from Tennessee by the name of

John and Zach show the bounties of their favorite activities (aside from boat-building)— John with ducks and Zach with crappie, circa 1996.

Pony Maples and no one can tell the story as well as John McClendon.

"Pony Maples is in the business of selling guns for military use. We had a contract with the Marine Corps in the works and we bought the guns for the boats from Pony—four guns per boat. When Pony came to fit the guns, he had a Toyota 4Runner with an eight-foot trailer on the back hauling a .50-caliber gun on a tripod.

"When the day's work was finished at SeaArk, they all drove down to the Camp for a visit and a couple of steaks. This was in the spring and all the fields around the Camp had been disked so the dirt was real loose. The sun was setting so before it got dark, Zach asked, 'Pony, when are you gonna let me shoot that fifty?' Pony said, 'Step outside, Mr. McClendon, and we'll light it up!'

"So they did. They backed the trailer up to the edge of the cotton field, Pony got the gun ready, and Zach hopped up on the trailer. It had a paddle trigger on it and Zach had all his ear protection on and he pushed that paddle and that thing went Boosh, Boosh, Boosh! He said he was shooting the thing at an angle—down into the dirt. About every third or fourth round was a phosphorous tracer so, of course, it looks like a laser beam going out there. But what happened was, it was going into the dirt and packing

it so hard that it started ricocheting straight up in the air. Zach said for thirty seconds or so, they didn't know what was going on. They heard timber cracking a mile and a half away at the end of our property. The only liquor store in our county is on the other side of that timber. They heard timber cracking and tracers going up in the air and everybody kind of freaked! So Zach said, 'How far will this thing go?' Pony said, 'Well, it's got an effective range of about four and a half miles.'

"Now, Zach really freaked. He ran inside and called the sheriff and said, 'Sheriff, if anybody complains about bullets flying around at the liquor store, call me.' Of course, it all worked out okay; the liquor store didn't get hit and no one got hurt. But it's been a legendary story around here for years."

Three generations of McClendons, ardent fans of hunting, fishing, and nature.

A Gift for Hospitality

To visit the McClendons' Camp is to experience firsthand virtually everything the family holds dear—friends, boats of all kinds, nature in general, good times, and most importantly, each other. Regardless of the nature of the hospitality, it is always freely extended and always genuine. "I just want people to feel welcome," Zach will tell you. And they do.

Business and friendship combine as dealer Jeff Miller (left) and family from Ocala, Florida, have visited for many years to duck hunt at Mink Track.

SeaArk Boats

Aluminum Jon Boats,
Super Jons,
Bass Boats
& Pontoon Boats

YOUR PARTNER FOR OUTDOOR ADVENTURES

1992 SeaArk Boats catalog.

Chapter Six

A BOAT COMPANY IS RECREATED

When Zach McClendon made the difficult decision to sell MonArk's recreational boat business to Brunswick, one half of the seesaw that helped MonArk maintain its balance during difficult economic times was gone. However, one product escaped Zach's non-compete agreement with Brunswick since it was not part of MonArk's product line at the time—houseboats. In 1989, Zach started up Sun River and for a time, small trailer-able houseboats were manufactured at a separate facility. Built on a pontoon chassis, the Sun River boats had hook-ups and connections that were compatible with campgrounds, making them a combination houseboat/recreational vehicle.

It was inevitable that Zach would find his way back to building the kind of boats that gave him his start. In the years that followed the sale to Brunswick and the family's re-emergence in the recreational boat business, SeaArk would see two more McClendons join the team.

Upon becoming acquainted with the McClendon family, the first thing you notice is their natural friendliness and warm welcome. The second thing you notice is their work ethic, mostly because the moments they spend not working are few and far between. Whether it stems from generations of industrious Scottish heritage, an innate drive to succeed, or simple passion for the work they do, the McClendons have a work ethic of monumental proportions. Both Robin and John recall that their conversations with Zach, even when they were young, almost always focused on accomplishing something. Said John, "He talked to us a lot about accomplishing our goals. You didn't *have* to do anything—you didn't have to play football or be an Eagle Scout—but if you started something, you had to finish it."

Yet for all his energy and determination, Zach also instilled the virtues of gratitude and compassion in his children. Said John, "Zach is a very fair person and a very gentle person. Robin and I were fortunate growing up but Zach always wanted us to be humble; he wanted us to be compassionate and have a lot of empathy for people who weren't as fortunate." Hard work, compassion, gratitude, and humility—these were the well-planted traits that would launch the next generation of SeaArk leadership.

Featured in the November 1990 issue of Sea Power, SeaArk built seven 35-foot Stinger Riverine Assault Crafts for the U.S. Marine Corps.

This 46-foot Transporter model was built and used by SeaArk to rescue stranded cattle during the 1990 flood.

The Great Cattle Rescue

Among the many values that Zach McClendon has passed on to Robin and John are his love of animals and respect for another person's labor. These two came together in a story of compassion and generosity, told by Robin McClendon.

"In the late spring of 1990, the Arkansas River was flooding well out of its banks. There was a cattle farmer who had grazing land near the river north of Pine Bluff. The rising water made it impossible for him to move his cattle to higher ground and the entire herd was in jeopardy of being drowned as the water continued to rise.

"SeaArk Marine had built a 46-foot Transporter, a powered barge with a landing craft-style ramp, for a state

park in California. The boat was twin diesel-powered and had a 20,000-pound payload capacity. It was complete and being readied for shipment when the river started to rise. We took it to Pine Bluff and launched it, along with a couple of smaller boats, and proceeded to take it up to where the cows were. Load after load of cattle were successfully relocated to higher ground and the farmer didn't lose a single animal.

"The only downside to this operation was that the cargo deck area of the barge was knee-deep in cow manure and required extensive cleaning before it could be shipped out to the customer in California."

Robin Joins the SeaArk Team

Robin graduated from Northeast Louisiana University in 1985, having majored in business administration. Following a short stint in the real estate business, she moved to Atlanta. She accepted a position as patient services coordinator for the Muscular Dystrophy Association and found herself enjoying big-city life. In 1989, Zach began recruiting her. "I had been over there a couple of times and visited with her and talked to her about coming back," Zach said. "I asked her if she would come over here and do the marketing for Marine."

SeaArk was using an outside ad agency for all of their advertising and catalogs and the challenge of working with "non-boat people" was proving to be frustrating. Robin explained, "If you don't know boats, it's hard to write ad copy and press releases." Zach called her and asked her if she wanted the job but, at first, she declined. "I loved Atlanta, but Zach is pretty persuasive. Several phone calls later, I agreed to come home." Though Robin's responsibilities stretched across a broad spectrum, most of her time was spent writing copy and designing ads, coordinating special events, and handling photo shoots.

SeaArk Boats

By 1992, Zach's non-compete agreement with Brunswick expired and with their Monticello plant closed, Zach saw an opportunity to get back into the recreational boat business. The start-up of the new SeaArk Boats varied from the start-up of the original MonArk Boat Company through one crucial difference—planning. One of the first people Zach called on was MonArk's former salesman, Dick Dickinson. Dick left MonArk in 1987 but rejoined the company on April 15, 1992, when Zach called him and asked him to help jumpstart the company. SeaArk Boats was incorporated just two days later. Dick recalled their planning sessions:

"One of the first things that Zach and I did was sit down and make a list. We not only listed every dealer we could think of, we listed every piece of equipment, and everything we would need to build boats again. Then we

A United States Marine Corps CH-53 Helicopter lifts a SeaArk Marine 35-foot Riverine Assault Craft (RAC) during a training exercise at Camp LeJeune, North Carolina, in the summer of 1991. Photo courtesy U.S. Marine Corps.

made a list of everything that could go wrong and every mistake we had ever made in the boat business, determined to have the perfect operation.

"Zach's goal was $1 million in sales the first year. We started the operation in a small shop at SeaArk Marine, having sold the recreational boat facility with the sale of MonArk. Zach hired Charles Carter to run production, the famous Prince brothers (Dennis and Roger who were known to turn out a phenomenal number of riveted boats a day), and Tommy Boyd, a welder from the MonArk days.

"But we needed a painter. Zach told me about Robert Benson, a longtime painter for MonArk who was then retired. I contacted Robert several times; each time Robert politely refused the job. Finally, I went to see Robert one day and sat on the porch all afternoon, just talking about fishing and visiting. As the sun began setting, I said, 'Robert, you know why I'm here. We need you to help us get started.' Robert agreed and came to work as SeaArk's painter-in-chief!"

Taking the post of president himself, Zach continued to round out his management team. Carl Ewell and Dennis Holley, already part of the team at SeaArk Marine, also joined SeaArk Boats as production supervisor of fabrication and manager of purchasing. Mike Thurman was design engineer and Jim Eoff, who was also with SeaArk Marine, was in charge of finance.

According to John, Zach made his intentions for this new company crystal clear to his new management team. John said that Zach announced, "Here's what we're going to do. We're going to build jon boats: two models of aluminum bass boats and two models of aluminum pontoon boats. That's all we're going to build. All I want is about fifteen dealers out there as customers. We're going to keep it small and keep it profitable." It was a perfectly rational, logical, and cautious plan that worked—for a while. Predictably, Zach's energy and creativity could not be contained, and within a year, they were offering roughly sixty models with multiple color schemes and had almost two hundred dealers on board.

Boats on Concrete

From MonArk's earliest days, they made a practice of teaming up with engine companies for their promotional photos. The first year that SeaArk Boats started up, they didn't have such a partner, so the new

SeaArk Boat models were photographed in the summer heat sitting on SeaArk's parking lot. As marketing director, Robin handled the photography and recruited friends and members of the SeaArk team who must have felt pretty foolish sitting in boats surrounded by concrete. "The photos did not look half bad after cropping out the concrete," Robin said, "and SeaArk Boats's first brochure was born just in time to go to the Dallas and Atlanta shows that fall." According to Robin, Dick Dickinson still has the memo that he sent to Zach after the Dallas and Atlanta shows. It lists sales of 349 jon boats, ninety-one bass boats, and thirty-three pontoons for a sales total of $647,063. As Dick said, "Not bad for only having the doors open six months!"

SeaArk Boats made the headlines of the *Advance Monticellonian* in June 1993 by building the world's largest jon boat, an occasion that caused Robin some consternation as the company's marketing director. Zach wanted to put a baby elephant in the boat for a photo shoot as a way of demonstrating the 24-foot-long and 96-inch-wide jon boat's capacity and stability. Robin recalled that Zach "never batted an eye that this may have been an odd or outrageous request" and acknowledges that Zach's "you never know until you ask" approach has gotten him more opportunities than most people would imagine. Despite her efforts at contacting several zoos, she wasn't able to get the erstwhile baby elephant and settled for putting a Dodge Neon in the boat to get the point across. Per Zach's suggestion, Robin also managed to fit three junior basketball teams in the same boat for another publicity shot.

SeaArk Marine

While things were firing up at SeaArk Boats, SeaArk Marine was anything but idle. In February 1992, they built three different models of boats for the Environmental Protection Agency. One was a 27-foot flat bottom to be used in the Great Lakes basin to search for toxic pollutants as part of a five-year study mandated by the Clean Water Act of 1987. The EPA used two other models as part of a long-term project to provide scientists and the public at large with information regarding the environmental health of waterways throughout the country.

Later that year, SeaArk Marine built three offshore, high-speed patrol boats for the Jamaican government. The 40-foot Dauntless class vessel was the first in a series of deep-vee hulls to be produced by SeaArk

SeaArk Boats made headlines in 1993 when it constructed the world's largest jon boat. To demonstrate the boat's capacity and stability, a Dodge Neon was used in one publicity shot and three basketball teams in another. SeaArk later sold two 2472s to an advertising firm for use in a national ad campaign for a major automobile manufacturer.

Lester Halbert (second from right) poses with the recipients of a new SeaArk Marine fireboat on the island of Batam near Indonesia during a training exercise in 1994.

Zach started up Sun River Marine after selling the recreational boat division to Brunswick. This brochure shows Susan McClendon, Zach's second wife, and Niels Skjerbeck. Susan was an integral part of the Drew Foam team and Niels ran Sun River after working in the Engineering Department at MonArk for many years.

Niels originally became acquainted with Zach, Sr. and Pauline during a trip to Denmark in the late 1960s. Niels was a driver for them while touring the country and Zach, Sr. was quite impressed with him. At the end of his trip, Zach, Sr. suggested that Niels contact him should he ever find himself in the States. Niels took him up on the offer, almost beating Zach and Pauline back!

Pauline McClendon, family matriarch, died in 1994. She was always very supportive of her family's business pursuits.

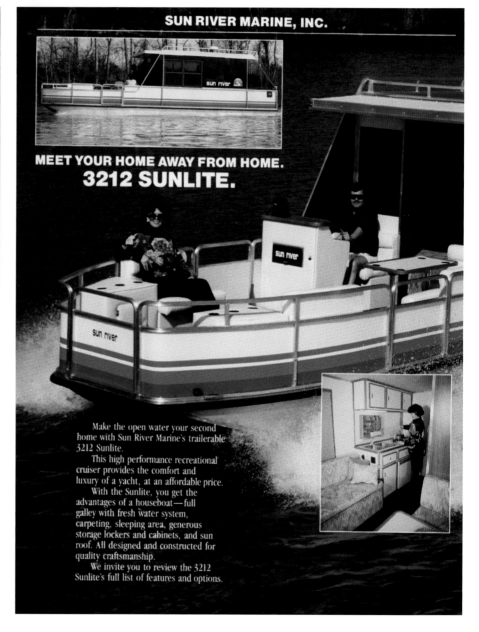

SUN RIVER MARINE, INC.

MEET YOUR HOME AWAY FROM HOME.
3212 SUNLITE.

Make the open water your second home with Sun River Marine's trailerable 3212 Sunlite.

This high performance recreational cruiser provides the comfort and luxury of a yacht, at an affordable price.

With the Sunlite, you get the advantages of a houseboat—full galley with fresh water system, carpeting, sleeping area, generous storage lockers and cabinets, and sun roof. All designed and constructed for quality craftsmanship.

We invite you to review the 3212 Sunlite's full list of features and options.

Buck Permenter (left) of the U.S. Army Corps of Engineers Memphis District and Cas Kirby, head engineer for SeaArk Marine, on board a 1970s-era MonArk workboat, discussing alterations to be made to the boat during a refurbish contract, circa 1995.

Marine and was made available in models from 28 to 44 feet in length and could be outfitted with firefighting systems as well. The vessel reported a trial speed of twenty-eight knots, giving it the capacity needed for use as an emergency response vessel.

John Comes On Board

John McClendon's first real job working for Zach was at E M & F, where he worked several summers starting at about the age of thirteen. He earned his degree in business administration from the University of Arkansas at Little Rock in 1992, having worked intermittently at both Sun River Marine and SeaArk Marine. John doesn't have particularly fond memories of the time he spent at Sun River, recalling the New Year's Eve in 1989 when midnight approached and he was still working, counting screws for the inventory.

John was working in Little Rock when Zach called him in 1994 to talk to him about coming to work at SeaArk. Sales at SeaArk Marine had been slumping and Zach wanted him to go to work in sales. John himself was surprised at how quickly he jumped at the chance.

Like many young people who grow up in a small town, John vowed he'd never go back to living there. "There is just something about this business and the family element that would not be denied," he said. "I had worked in the workboat shops every summer," and boats had been a part of his life since he was a young boy. "As we say in the boat business, I had webbed feet."

When John arrived at SeaArk Marine in May 1994, he was hired as a sales trainee. Since the sell-off of MonArk's Recreational Division in 1988, SeaArk Marine had lost money four of the previous six years and as John says, "It was the worst of times to learn the business." The year before, Robert Trammel left SeaArk Marine and Zach took on the presidency of both SeaArk Marine and SeaArk Boats on top of his responsibilities at Drew Foam and Union Bank. Johnny Smith, vice president of sales, had also left the company, though both he and Robert Trammel were occasionally available for special projects.

John immediately got busy on the road. "There was nowhere I wouldn't (or didn't) go to try and sell a boat. So far I've been to twenty-seven different countries

Zach looks on as a U.S. Coast Guard commander gives the opening remarks during the christening ceremony in Little Rock for the first of nine 40-footers bound for service in the Caribbean, May 1995.

A SeaArk Marine 42-foot Dauntless is caught on film by the U.S. Coast Guard during the rescue of over seventy-five Haitian refugees off the coast of Florida. Photo courtesy U.S. Coast Guard.

Johnny Smith and Robert Trammel are flanked by Marine Corps officials aboard a 35-foot Riverine Assault Craft. Johnny worked at MonArk and then SeaArk Marine for more than twenty years. His efforts helped the Monticello boat builder become a key provider of military vessels to countries throughout the world. Robert helped guide the company with the transition from MonArk to SeaArk and continues to this day as financial advisor to the McClendon family.

and every U.S. state except Hawaii. Peru, Colombia, Japan, Egypt—it didn't matter; I was there pressing the flesh with some junior grade lieutenant, the king's first cousin, and everyone in between."

John reported to Ken McFalls, who was serving as sales manager at the time. His first sale was to the U.S. Forest Service in Alaska, a simple Transporter. Shortly thereafter, he sold five boats to the Coast Guard in Alaska, a 32-foot crew boat to the National Park Service in coastal Georgia, and in 1995, he landed a contract for thirty-six boats for the Alabama Marine Police. The boats for Alabama were based on a design for a law enforcement boat that John devised in conjunction with SeaArk's engineer Cas Kirby and Bill Garner of the Alabama Marine Police.

One of the biggest contracts at the time, one that gave SeaArk a big boost, was a NAVSEA contract for their 40-foot Dauntless class patrol boat. Though the initial contract was for nine boats, SeaArk Marine ulti-

mately built fourteen boats for drug interdiction along the coasts of Trinidad and the eastern Caribbean islands. Regional dignitaries were on hand for the christening of the first of the nine boats on the Arkansas River in Little Rock. State Senator Jim Scott, U.S. Congressman Jay Dickey, Arkansas Governor Jim Guy Tucker, and Drew County Judge Garland McAnally joined Zach McClendon in a tour of the boat following the ceremony.

SeaArk's contracts with the Navy proved to be lucrative; however, their practice of paying for the boats in milestone payments, to be paid in increments as the boats completed each phase of their construction, created a cash flow challenge for SeaArk. Robert Trammel, a former SeaArk president and the company's outside accountant at the time, helped John secure the funds to finance the project. Without Robert's help, that financing probably would not have come through, and his influence was a tremendous help to SeaArk.

SeaArk Marine entered the Rigid Hull Inflatable market for the first time in 1995. Paul Hureau, who had previously run Boston Whaler's commercial products division, was recruited to SeaArk Marine around 1990 to help develop such models and refine the entire product line.

One of Hureau's first major contributions was to introduce the SeaArk engineering team to C. Raymond Hunt & Associates, the world-renowned naval architecture firm that would develop the extremely popular Commander and Dauntless class deep-vees for SeaArk Marine. The Hureau-SeaArk-Hunt relationship remains strong and successful to this day.

John, Robin, and Zach McClendon, Jr. during a Navy commissioning ceremony in Little Rock in May 1995.

Excursion Boats

SeaArk Marine's excursion boat line grew out of some experimental projects at Sun River, starting with the excursion boats they built for Hammocks Beach State Park in North Carolina in 1990. When operations at Sun River were shut down, SeaArk Marine picked up the product line and developed two different models, the Olympia and the Explorer.

The Olympia, similar to the boats mentioned above, was Coast Guard-certified for forty passengers. SeaArk Marine built eight of these excursion boats for the 1996 Olympic games in Atlanta. Many of the water events were held in nearby Savannah and the boats were used to transport athletes, judges, and production crews out to the artificial "island" that was built out in the sound specifically for these events.

SeaArk Marine also built the Explorer model, a larger excursion boat certified for ninety passengers, for customers in North Carolina, Florida, and Washington State. Many of these boats were used in the mid-1990s for "eco tours" long before they became fashionable putting SeaArk, however unwittingly, on the cutting edge of the environmental movement.

In 1995, SeaArk Marine built thirty excursion boats for Yanaguana Cruises, Inc. of San Antonio, Texas. Having been awarded the ten-year boat ride concession for the city's famous River Walk on the San Antonio River, they placed an order for ten more boats for delivery the following year. The excursion boats were built to run on environmentally friendly compressed natural gas, eliminating much of the noise, odor, and smoke associated with two-stroke gasoline engines.

SeaArk Marine's success with excursion boats sparked Zach to start up yet another business—the International Waterfront Group. It was a sound idea whose success was unfortunately tied to one of those people that, according to John, Zach "attracts like a magnet." The venture wasn't long-lived, but the excursion boats remain part of SeaArk Marine's product line to this day, having built hundreds of them for cities and amusement parks across the country.

Patton Street

In September 1996, SeaArk Boats moved its production from SeaArk Marine into the plant on Patton Street that had originally been the site of MonArk Boats. Brunswick occupied the plant following their purchase of the MonArk recreational business, and since 1991, the Amfuel Division of Zodiac USA occupied it. Although Zodiac wasn't making boat-related products at the plant, their parent company was a direct competitor to SeaArk Marine. The irony of coming back to this location, with a competitor in between, is not lost on the McClendons. Zach was quoted in the June 9, 1996 edition of the *Commercial Appeal* in Memphis, saying, "It feels good to be going back to the old plant. We have most of our people again. We've come full circle."

In 1997, Don Law was named president of both SeaArk Boats and SeaArk Marine. The same year, John became the manager of the quality assurance department for both SeaArk Boats and SeaArk Marine. Lester Halbert—for whom John had worked in 1990—was the supervisor of this department and tended to its day-to-day activities; John was charged with the task of improving all aspects of SeaArk's product quality and customer relations.

OMC Lawsuit

In manufacturing, you know you're doing something right when the competition comes after you, like the time that SeaArk Boats introduced a deck boat to their product line in 1995. It was a bit unique in that it had an aluminum bottom but then was decked out like a pontoon. At the time, OMC (Outboard Marine Corporation), manufacturers of Johnson and Evinrude engines, started buying up boat companies much the same way Brunswick had purchased MonArk years earlier.

One of the many boat companies owned by OMC had a deck boat model with a bridge system that had

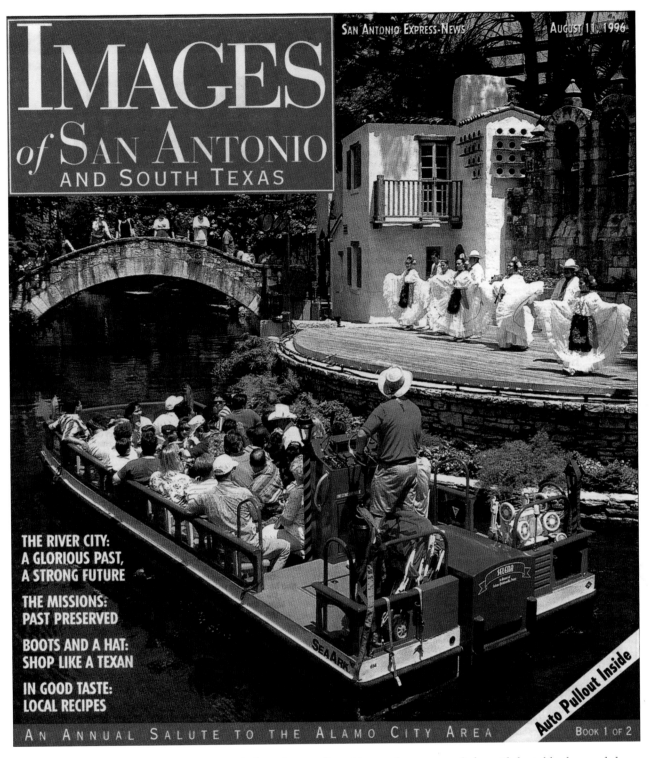

Within the image:

The River Walk in San Antonio, Texas, attracts about eleven million visitors each year, many of whom ride boats like these made by SeaArk Marine. Powered by environmentally friendly compressed natural gas, the boats' success has resulted in similar riverwalk projects being developed by Oklahoma City and Richmond, Virginia. Reprinted with permission from the San Antonio Express-News.

four risers to support the deck. OMC came up with a similar design a couple of years prior that hadn't really gained popularity until about the time SeaArk came out with their deck boat. Any similarity between the boats was purely coincidental and, as John explained, "We came up with the same deck riser support because it was the logical way to construct the boat." Nonetheless, to squelch SeaArk's production, OMC claimed that SeaArk was infringing on their patent rights.

SeaArk's attorney told them they could win the case. However, as in all things legal, it was going to cost them. In the end, SeaArk settled the case, tweaked their design just enough to bypass OMC's patented design, and moved on. As in years earlier, the legal challenge only fu-

The McClellan-Kerr Waterway Flotilla

In 1996, the McClellan-Kerr waterway system celebrated the twenty-fifth anniversary of the locks and dams by coordinating a flotilla to commemorate the flotilla held during the original dedication in 1971. Pontoons and yachts of all sizes were included as they floated the Arkansas River from Tulsa to Dumas over a ten-day period. Each port town along the way provided a celebration for the participants.

Some of the participating boats were too large to anchor at shore, so the Arkansas Waterway Commission asked SeaArk Boats to provide boats to shuttle the passengers to shore each night for the celebrations. SeaArk Boats agreed and provided four boats, among them a "Water Taxi" specially designed for hauling up to twenty-four people at a time along with two deck boats. The fourth boat was the Garfish, a big jon boat outfitted with a large fuel tank for refueling the SeaArk fleet and tools, two-way radios, and other equipment that might be needed. The Garfish came to the rescue more than once for participants in the flotilla.

Providing boats was much easier than providing crews for them and the logistics involved in getting SeaArk's people in and out of the flotilla proved to be the bigger challenge. Robin McClendon, who handled that logistical challenge, recalled the event:

"John and I were the only ones from SeaArk to participate the entire ten days. We had plenty of staff members willing to volunteer but we couldn't have them away from their 'real' jobs for that length of time so we scheduled them for two- to four-day periods. That required a master schedule of vehicles back and forth from Monticello. A huge amount of planning went into the gear required for each boat. We needed rain ponchos, fire extinguishers, tools, flashlights, fresh water, and anything

else that might be needed for ten days on the river. We had uniforms to keep the SeaArk crew looking professional. People needed hotel rooms along the way and we had vehicles following the entire trip on land to take us to hotel rooms and bring food provisions for the meals that weren't provided during the celebrations.

"Planning for this event was one of the most time-consuming and complicated things I've ever worked on. Even still, it was one of the most enjoyable experiences I've had. I LOVED going down that river, locking through the locks and meeting people in all the towns."

Once on the river, there were some challenges, to be sure. Quickly realizing they could not run directly behind the big yachts because of the wake, they either tried to get out in front of them or give them an hour head start. They often had to wait several hours to lock through since any commercial traffic had priority. Of course, SeaArk folks know how to make the best of things, and spent the time on a sandbar swimming and fishing. Sometimes the people proved to be the biggest challenge of all.

Most of the people they shuttled were very nice and one of Robin's favorite communities dropped boxed lunches down to them as they locked through as their part of the celebration. But the highlight for Robin was having the opportunity to meet Alice Guffey Miller, the artist whose sculpture made completely out of recycled materials was transported on a Corps of Engineers Education Barge. Discovering that she also lived in Monticello, they became good friends, and Robin counts Alice and her husband Gary Marshall among her dearest friends. Alice was recently chosen to do a set of sculptures for the Historic Arkansas Museum in Little Rock and the half-inch aluminum that she plans to use will be cut at SeaArk.

A gentleman named Phil Leonard, who participated in the original dedication in 1971, developed some engine malfunctions on his boat in the 1996 flotilla. When John refilled his fuel tanks out on the waterway and refused to accept any payment, Phil was moved to write a letter to a local paper, saying, "If I should ever have a need for a real classy boat I will certainly contact SeaArk. My crew and I again thank them for their kindness and generosity."

The SeaArk team provided a shuttle service for participants in the flotilla commemorating the twenty-fifth anniversary of the opening of the McClellan-Kerr waterway system, 1996.

Robin talks with dealer Phil Rose at a "traveling show" in Illinois, 2004.

eled SeaArk's determination to succeed. And, it should be noted, OMC went out of business a few years later.

Boat Shows

Over the past fifty years, MonArk and SeaArk have attended literally hundreds of different trade, consumer, and dealer shows.

Most dealers who sell the recreational products offered by MonArk/SeaArk participate in consumer "boat shows." These shows offer the opportunity to show the dealers' lines and often end with many sales for the dealer. Although the manufacturers don't officially display at these shows, sales reps and company personnel usually attend the larger ones to support the dealer and help with answering the endless questions that consumers have about the products on display.

Trade shows, another type of boat show, were a vital part of the recreational boat industry up until the early 1990s. These shows were not open to the public and were designed for manufacturers to show their new products for the next model year to their dealers. It was also the place where most of the new business was generated, meaning new dealers for

A SeaArk Boats "in-water" show held in Hot Springs, Arkansas, in 2005.

the line. Manufacturers purchased display space and set up a huge "booth" to show their product line. There were usually one or two major shows a year and if you wanted your line to be known, you had to be there. Though it was very convenient to have most of the dealers under one roof at the same time, the big trade shows were not without their share of challenges.

The typical show starts several days before the event opens to the attendees. Truckloads of boats arrive at the exposition location and a team from the home office, sometimes joined by regional sales representatives, begins the set-up. Temporary carpet is laid, boats are put into place on foam blocks using furniture dollies, and often an elaborate sales and meeting area consisting of everything down to a telephone and live plants is arranged in the booth. The entire set-up process is reversed after three days of the trade show and the booth is completely disassembled and boats loaded back up to ship out.

The actual set-up takes place fast (but often after many hours of standing around waiting) under the combined oversight of show organizers and convention hall union labor. Booth restrictions and show

SeaArk Marine produced the sleek Desert Shadow *in 1996. The 85-foot aluminum passenger vessel was delivered to Aramark Leisure Services in Page, Arizona. The U.S. Coast Guard certified the boat to transport 149 passengers. Courtesy of Aramark Leisure Services.*

criteria can border on the comical. Rarely do things go according to schedule or as planned during the set-up and tear-down of a show, and one has to remain flexible as hundreds of competitors and vendors construct their temporary showrooms all around you.

Once the show opens, a grueling marathon begins of nearly constant standing and talking, after-show client entertaining that can last late into the night, and redirecting vendors and other "non-buying" people away from the booth. Shows are generally very expensive and short in duration. The object is to maximize every minute of time, focusing on attracting potential buyers to the company and selling the new season's models to existing dealers.

The most notable and longest lasting of the trade shows was the International Marine Trade Exhibition and Conference (IMTEC) usually held at McCormick Place in Chicago. Zach remembers the worst of all shows was during the late 1960s: "McCormick Place in Chicago had a fire prior to the dates of the show that year. The show organizers moved it to Detroit as a result. The first day of the show it started snowing. By mid-day on the second day there was three feet of snow outside and you could have fired a shotgun down the aisles inside that place and not hit living thing. I don't think we sold a single boat at the show that year. It was awful."

After the big trade shows like IMTEC died off, manufacturers were left with no way to display new products to dealers. This is when the "dealer show" was born. Manufacturers started holding very short two- or three-day shows specifically for the purpose of showing boats to a captive audience. These shows were usually held at an in-water location so boats could be test-driven by the dealers in attendance. These shows are expensive and labor-intensive to stage, but the rewards can be big if the dealers place big orders at the show.

Occasionally, employees, customers, competitors, and vendors alike forget their manners at a show or treat the opportunity as a vacation. Once during a dealer show in the early 1990s, a display boat was noted as overdue from a test drive. Several employees were dispatched in demonstration boats to try and locate the missing dealer and boat. He was found some hours later, passed out drunk on the floor of the boat, floating aimlessly in the middle of the lake.

By 2001, the economic slump made it difficult for many dealers to attend the shows. For the next few years, SeaArk Boats conducted a traveling boat show, holding one-day mini-shows that made it more affordable for dealers to attend. As business picked up, SeaArk Boats went back to the traditional dealer shows, where boats are staged on both land and water and include activities, entertainment, and good food—all the things for which the McClendons are known. Business meetings are held where dealers are presented awards based on their sales performance during the year. In recent years, SeaArk Boats's dealer show has been lauded among the best in the industry.

There is also a trade show for the workboat side of the business. The International Workboat Show held in New Orleans each year offers builders and suppliers to the industry the opportunity to get together as well as show off their products to potential customers. SeaArk Marine has displayed boats every year for the last several years and counts this as an important function for obtaining new business.

In addition to the Workboat Show, MonArk/SeaArk has participated in numerous industry-related expos and conferences over the years, including the Offshore Technology Conference (OTC), Oil Spill Events, LAGCOE (Louisiana Gulf Coast Oil Expo), and the Multi-Agency Craft Conference, also known as the MACC Show. The MACC conference, held in Norfolk, Virginia, is sponsored by NAVSEA for the purpose of bringing marine industry and government agencies together to foster new insight and creative ideas that will further the advancement of marine and military-used products.

Regardless of the type, boat shows are undeniably a lot of work to stage and often come with a hefty price tag, but they are a very necessary part of the boat business.

SeaArk Pride

It was almost time for the next generation of McClendons to take the lead at SeaArk, but before they did, two projects came into play that brought a lot of pride to the company, along with a few headaches.

One was the *Desert Shadow*, an 85-foot passenger motor yacht that SeaArk Marine built in 1996 for Aramark Leisure Services, the concessionary for Glen Canyon National Recreation Area, for use on Lake Powell, Arizona. The boat was built in Monticello and trucked to Arizona. The shipping cost alone was over $50,000. "This project was a huge money loser," John recalled, "but one that Zach wanted to do very badly and we did it. He is still to this day extremely proud of that boat." Except for Aramark's 91-foot paddle wheeler, the *Desert Shadow* was the largest boat in their fleet.

The other project had its own cryptic code name: The Zulu Project. A story in itself, it was one of those projects that Zach felt strongly about and his decision to take on the project was guided not by financial gain but by Zach's desire to tackle a challenging project for the sake of proving just exactly how much his SeaArk team was capable of doing. He was right on both counts: the project wasn't profitable, but it definitely turned out to be a feather in SeaArk's cap.

Sources:
Harper, Kim. "A big fish in a small town." *Arkansas Business*, Feb. 3, 1992.
Maritime Reporter, November 1992.

The Zulu Project

One of SeaArk's most interesting projects even had its own code name: The Zulu Project. Not many companies have the opportunity to build a boat for an extremely wealthy yacht enthusiast. This gentleman (who must remain anonymous) originally ordered a 40-foot dive boat for his daughter from a competitor in Seattle. Not satisfied with the boat's speed, he eventually sued the manufacturer who had, by then, gone out of business. SeaArk had recently hired Mike Caldwell, who had previously worked for this particular competitor. Mike convinced the wealthy customer to let SeaArk work on the boat to bring it up to snuff. The wealthy customer, thrilled with SeaArk's work on the dive boat, then ordered another boat from SeaArk.

As it happened, business was slow, but this project was complicated. The boat had a lot of specifications and restrictions and some features that were new to the engineers at SeaArk. Zach brought everyone who had any capacity for decision-making into the conference room to discuss the pros and cons of taking on the project. It became obvious that Zach alone wanted to tackle the project and the discussion eventually escalated into an argument. Finally, Zach said, "We're going to do this democratically! Everyone who doesn't want to do this project, raise your hand." To a man, everyone but Zach raised his hand, voting not to take it on. Upon seeing this, Zach said, "Sign the contract—let's get this thing started!"

The boat was built to the customer's satisfaction complete with custom-molded, shock-mitigating seats that cost $16,000 each. It didn't turn out to be a profitable venture for SeaArk, but then Zach McClendon's decision-making process isn't always profit-motivated. To his credit, it's sometimes about the challenge, and sometimes about keeping the doors open and people working. And when Zach sets his mind to do something…

Officials chose one of SeaArk's RAM class patrol boats to escort the 200-year-old USS Constitution during her historic 1997 sail in Boston Harbor. The forty-four-gun frigate, nicknamed Old Ironsides, was first launched in 1797 and became one of the most famous vessels in U.S. naval history.

The McClendons put their trademark touches on commissioning ceremony party favors with custom-labeled champagne bottles and cans of armadillo meat.

A label from a can of armadillo meat: "Packaged for SeaArk's Best Customers."

Serving Suggestions:
Best when spread on a cracker and served with RC Cola and a Moon Pie.

PURE ARKANSAS ARMADILLO

Sun Dried & Road Tenderized

A Product of Arkansas
Ingredients: Pure Sun Dried Armadillo run over by a log truck 7 miles South of Monticello, Arkansas. Not over 20% hair, gravel, wood chips, and foreign matter.

Net Wt. 3 oz.

SeaArk MARINE

PACKAGED FOR SeaArk'S BEST CUSTOMERS

Naval Coastal Warfare Group 2 during a deployment exercise at Little Creek Amphibious Base, Norfolk, Virginia, in 2003. Photo courtesy of U.S. Navy.

The SeaArk Marine 34-foot Naval Coastal Warfare boats feature a .50-caliber machine gun in the forward gun tub. Photo courtesy of U.S. Navy.

SeaArk Boats

ALUMINUM JONS, SUPER JONS, DUCK HUNTING BOATS, FISHING MODELS & DECK STYLE BOATS

Year 2000 Boat Models

BayFisher

DuckHawk 1652-DD

1652-PCC

ZX200-DC

ZV177

Sun Tastic

We Love to Fish SeaArk Boats

P. O. Box 803
Monticello, Arkansas 71657, U.S.A.
870-367-5317 • Fax: 870-460-3200
www.seaark.com
www.aluminumboat.com

2000 SeaArk Boats catalog.

Chapter Seven

A NEW GENERATION AT THE HELM

It's a safe assumption that anyone who starts and then builds a family-owned business dreams not only of what that business can provide for his or her family, but also the day when that family would step up to the front office. That day was about to arrive.

Don Law worked for MonArk from 1975 to 1985 and much of the company's success in those years can be attributed to Don's achievements in marketing and sales. He left MonArk for a time and rejoined the team as president of both SeaArk Marine and SeaArk Boats in February 1997. When John McClendon was named president of SeaArk Marine in 1998, Don Law was promoted to chairman and continued his post as president of SeaArk Boats.

John was promoted to president of SeaArk Marine on June 1, 1998. The first year of John's presidency was still not profitable for SeaArk Marine, since many of the projects that were still in the production pipeline were costly projects with little profit margin. However, by the end of his second year as president in 2000, SeaArk returned to the profit side of business and they have posted a profit each year since then. The company has achieved several significant records during this time, including the highest all-time net income of any year in 2003, the highest all-time sales volume in 2004, and the highest all-time recognized revenue in 2007.

"To say I am proud of this accomplishment is an understatement," John says, "but truly it has less to do with what little talent I may possess, and more to do with cutting the overhead down, focusing on profitable projects, and most importantly building a good team."

John freely admits that while Robin inherited a measure of Zach's entrepreneurial daring, he inherited his grandfather's calculating, cautious approach to business. All of them acknowledge that having both sides of the entrepreneurial coin to draw upon is ideal, particularly in today's more complicated business climate. As John reflected, "In MonArk's early days, if the boat business hadn't worked out they would have shut it down and gone on to something else. With today's government regulations and the standards imposed by the boat industry itself, starting up a business like this would involve a tremendous outlay of capital. The stakes are so much higher now than they were in 1958."

John's approach to the business reflects this fundamental change in the industry. "Early on, their strategy was somewhat reactionary, saying to the customer, 'Tell us what you want and we'll build it.' That was fine

Another McClendon at the wheel. Johnny, John's son and the grandson of Zach, took to boats at an early age. Courtesy of the McClendon family.

John McClendon speaks at the commissioning ceremony of a SeaArk Marine 57-foot Dauntless built for the Port of South Louisiana, August 2007.

A SeaArk Marine 32-foot Dauntless with members of the East Baton Rouge Parish Sheriff's Department SWAT Team, 2007. Courtesy of East Baton Rouge Parish Sheriff's Department.

at first, but the product kept getting more complicated and our competition's capabilities were increasing ahead of ours. My goal in this organization was to get ahead of that, to go to the customer and say, 'Tell us what you want to do and we'll help you figure out which of our boats will meet your needs.'

"To his credit, Zach's mentality was to take on projects, even if they weren't going to be terribly profitable, in order to keep the doors open and keep people working," John said. Years later, SeaArk Marine's success affords him the luxury of being able to "cherry pick" the projects that will be profitable while saying "no" to the rest.

Marine News interviewed John when he became the new president of SeaArk Marine in 1999 and he noted the company's investment in SeaArk's technology base with the in-house computerized plasma cutter and "the most advanced aluminum deep-vee designs available." When asked how the market has changed over the past decade, John noted the company's shift from government back to a private sector company base and

Robin, like Zach, loves to fish and spend time on the water.

The BayRunner was one of many successful examples of turning a jon boat into a more specific fishing rig for SeaArk Boats.

The Predator, a sport jet boat, was introduced specifically for the Alaskan market, circa 2004.

with eerie accuracy, forecasted that the coming decade would bring "a slight shift back to government contracts as turmoil around the world escalates." Asked to name the three top issues that drive SeaArk's product development, John answered, "customer requirements, customer requirements, customer requirements."

Fortieth Anniversary

When SeaArk celebrated its fortieth anniversary in 1999, SeaArk Boats's product line included bass boats, crappie boats, sport fishing boats, tunnel hulls, and deck boats. In just seven short years, they had a loyal customer base of dealers across the United States, largely on the strength of the original MonArk name and reputation.

Trademarks

Just before a boat gets sent off for final rigging, many of them get shot inside with a layer of Gator Hide, a plastic rubber finish for which Zach copyrighted the name. The nubby surface gives SeaArk's recreational boats a more skid-proof surface and provides extra sound deadening.

Another of Zach's trademarked designs is Duck Brush Camo, a camouflage pattern he designed specifically for boats used for duck hunting.

Zach's unquenchable love of houseboats reared up again with the introduction in 1999 of the Voyager 25 trailer-able houseboat. SeaArk Boats built the 26-foot houseboat with an eight-foot, six-inch beam that allowed it to be towed without special permits and could also be used on land as a camper—a smaller version of the boats Zach previously built under the Sun River name. Losing interest after the initial design and production challenges were resolved, Zach sold the design. The new owner built the Voyagers in Monticello for a time and then moved the operation to Missouri, though SeaArk Boats continues to build the hulls for him to this day.

Robin Takes the Helm at SeaArk Boats

Robin McClendon had been in charge of the marketing for both SeaArk companies since the start-up of SeaArk Boats. In 1999, she was promoted to Vice President of Marketing and Communications. The following year, Charles Clinard became president of SeaArk Boats upon Don Law's retirement. Charles had previously worked with such companies as Glastron Boats, OMC, and Landau Boats, a company he owned and operated from 1989 to 1997. Charles was president of SeaArk Boats from August of 1999 until March of 2001.

Robin reflected on the turn of events leading up to her position as president of SeaArk Boats: "The company had not been profitable since we re-entered the recreational market in 1992. We hired several different people to run the company but had not had a family member involved in the day-to-day opera-

SeaArk Boats clears up rumors

Monticello, Arkansas

SeaArk Boats has announced plans to continue in the recreational boat building business indefinitely. The company had recently looked into several options including selling and suspending operations, but has made the decision to continue building recreational aluminum boats.

"Another rumor we have heard is that we had converted our operation to build work boats for the government," McClendon comments. "This is another incorrect report. It is true that our sister company, SeaArk Marine, has been awarded several large military contracts, but we have not combined any operations, and their facilities and production are completely independent of ours."

Dick Dickenson is vice president and Robin McClendon is president of SeaArk Boats

"We would like to put an end to all of the rumors going around," says Robin McClendon, president of SeaArk Boats. "We have not shut our doors, we have not sold out, and we have no plans to do either. Like most builders in our industry, we experienced some tough months after September 11. Contrary to rumors we have heard, we never shut down other than our normal Christmas week shutdown in December."

The company has made some changes to their product line, including concentrating on large all-welded jons and a line of bay boats. Until recently, SeaArk Boats built more than 75 different models of jons, deck style boats, and fishing boats. "By concentrating on 52-, 60-, and 72-inch bottom boats, we are targeting our niche markets," McClendon says.

SeaArk's 2003 product line was introduced July 1, 2002. Plans include the introduction of several new models and many added options and accessories.

McLendon also pointed out that SeaArk Boats should not be confused with its sister company, SeaArk Marine. SeaArk Marine is also located in Monticello, Arkansas, and builds work and patrol boats for the U. S. Government and for commercial use by private industry.

SeaArk Boats was started in 1992 by the McClendon family who founded and owned MonArk Boat Company for many years. After the sale of the recreational division of MonArk to Brunswick in 1988, the family retained the commercial workboat division and renamed it SeaArk Marine. Four years later, when a non-compete agreement for recreational product production expired, SeaArk Boats was created as a separate corporation.

"Our family has been building boats since 1959," says McClendon. "We plan on continuing this tradition for many years to come."

After taking the helm at SeaArk Boats, Robin's major obstacle was overcoming rumors about the company. Reprinted with permission from Boat & Motor Dealer.

SeaArk Boats introduced the Big Daddy, a 24-foot, 15-degree hull designed for fishing. MonArk/SeaArk often used employees and their family members as models. Shown here are Kristen Baker (Angela Naron's daughter), Mike Featherston (SeaArk Boats quality assurance manager), and Mike's wife, Cindy.

tions up to this point. In early 2001, then-president Charles Clinnard, who had been with us for only a little over a year, resigned. Zach asked me if I wanted the job. I said yes."

Robin knew immediately what challenges lay ahead for her. "Things were not in good shape. Fifty percent of our sales were to Travis Boating Centers. Travis was a giant of retail boat sales located in nine states throughout the south. Because they had become such a big customer, we were in a situation where they were squeezing us to the point where our margins were terrible. Then 9/11 hit."

By December 2001, things were looking very dire at SeaArk Boats. Robin knew that some painful choices had to be made, so she laid out an action plan for putting the company back on track.

Her first step was to declare a major lay-off of employees, an extremely difficult decision right before the Christmas holidays. She interviewed every single employee to determine if and where they might fit into the streamlined company. The number of employees was reduced from about 120 to about thirty-five. The more experienced and talented workers went over to SeaArk Marine. The rest were laid off.

The benefit, of course, was that their workforce was now the proverbial cream of the crop. As Robin said, "We had little need for supervision or even a quality assurance inspector. Everyone pitched in and did what they needed to do to save the company. It was really one of the most efficient times of production for us."

The next step was to re-examine the product line. Knowing that the company's bread-and-butter product had long been its big jon boats, she eliminated the deck boats and bass boats from the product line and focused

on their niche. As a result, she was able to reduce the inventory and eliminate some items completely. The reduced product line may have cost them a few dealers, but there was a positive aspect as well. Robin elaborated, "The dealers who focused on our jon boats got better quality boats and they got them faster. We were more focused and became very efficient." Their newfound success has often been based on a simple question: "What can we do or add to a jon boat to make it better?"

In a rather daring move, Robin severed the financially draining relationship with Travis Boating Centers. "We just could not sell boats any longer for those low profits and now with a smaller team and limited product line could not supply them anyway," she explained. As it turned out, the break with Travis would have been inevitable. Shortly thereafter, Johnny Morris, who owned Tracker Marine, purchased Travis, and since he also owned Fisher Boats, both manufacturers of aluminum boats, SeaArk's product line would likely have been dropped.

By severing the relationship with Travis, Robin got rid of the cripplingly low profit margins and was now free to concentrate on servicing independent dealers.

"We pushed our quality, which was definitely something that we had over other brands." Soon after the split with Travis, Robin had to call on her marketing and communications experience to refute rumors that SeaArk Boats had gone out of business or were now only building commercial boats for their sister company, SeaArk Marine.

The final step was to control inventory and waste. Said Robin, "We did everything we could to use what we had, reduce large purchases, and eliminate unnecessary spending. Years of poor control had created lots of obsolete inventory. We found ways to use up what was already purchased. We got tight with everything, even office supplies. I remember that we started using the back of paper to make copies for internal documents, so we would not have to purchase as much new paper." Other costs were cut as well. Instead of participating in the costly dealer shows, they went on the road marketing their boats to independent dealers by way of traveling mini-shows.

With the streamlined smaller team working together and the changes that were made, SeaArk Boats was able to slowly get back to being a major player in the aluminum recreational market. Robin is proud to say, "We have since expanded our team, our product line, and our dealer base, and now offer bass boats

SeaArk Boats' ProCat 240, designed by engineer Mark Tucker with the help of professional cat fishing guide Steve Brown.

SeaArk Boats found a niche with the cat fishing market and now makes several models of cat fishing boats.

and family-style boats once again. I am proud to say that since 2002, we have been in the black. We owe a lot to our team who suffered through our scale-down and raise freezes to get us back to profitability and the market share that we enjoy today."

Like John, Robin is quick to give credit where it's due and much of SeaArk Boats' success can be traced to Steve Henderson. When the Travis chain began to decline, Steve approached Robin. His family had once had retail boat stores in Pine Bluff and Little Rock.

When Travis bought them out, Steve went to work for the new owners. "I told Steve I needed to add to our inside sales team and he joined us," Robin said. "Since he grew up in the dealership business, he understood dealers' needs. He has been a big part of why we have been successful."

The philosophies that Robin developed in those early years have carried into the present. "We try to do what we do best and focus on that," she said. However, the company is constantly looking at ways to improve and "redevelop" their product. Taking the almost flat bottom jon boats, they have created several lines of special-purpose fishing boats. Having several other model hulls with deeper-vee designs, they have been able to create an expanded line of boats that work for dealers from Houston to Vermont to Alaska. "We try to listen to our dealers and study the market to see what might be a need out there," Robin said. "One of our dealers in Missouri said he had more and more people buying our boats for cat fishing because they're tough and durable. So, we came out with the Rivercat. It was a hit with people who did other kinds of fishing and wanted a big open boat." The Rivercat was SeaArk Boats's best-selling model in 2008. Since then, they've added a Vcat and a ProCat to the model line, which was designed with the help of a professional cat fishing guide. "The cat fishing market has become huge," Robin observed.

A Changed World

In October 2000, al-Qaeda terrorists bombed the USS *Cole*, a Navy destroyer, while it was harbored in the Yemeni port of Aden. Most Americans regarded it as a tragic but singular act of insanity—until September 11, 2001. On that day, the world watched the morning news shows in horror as terrorists flew planes into the towers of the World Trade Center in New York and the Pentagon. Not to be forgotten, another plane was seized by passengers and heroically crash-landed on a field near Shanksville, Pennsylvania.

The entire world looked different to us after that day. The continental United States had not been invaded since the War of 1812 but following the attacks of 9/11, homeland security was on everyone's minds. Federal and state agencies across the country beefed up their security.

By 2002, SeaArk Marine's primary business was to domestic government customers such as the U.S. Navy, U.S. Coast Guard, U.S. Army Corps of Engineers, and U.S. Border Patrol.

In 2002, SeaArk Marine delivered two 65-foot survey boats to the U.S. Army Corps of Engineers New Orleans District. The Dauntless deep-vee was designed to perform hydrographic survey missions for the Corps of Engineers along the lower Mississippi River and its tributaries, as well as in the Gulf of Mexico. Earlier that year, SeaArk delivered a multi-boat order for Naval Sea Systems Command (NAVSEA) to be added to its Pacific fleet for harbor security.

As of December 2002, SeaArk had orders for forty-two of their 27-foot Commander-class harbor security boats for NAVSEA's Atlantic fleet. Also in 2002, SeaArk was awarded a $14-million contract from NAVSEA for thirty-six coastal warfare boats to be delivered over a two-year period.

When the Naval Force Protection boats were built, a process that took approximately four months from start to finish, they were taken to the Arkansas River at Pine Bluff for testing. Lester Halbert, SeaArk's quality assurance manager, put the boats through approximately twenty tests, a two-day pro-

CNO Admiral Gary Roughhead (on right) on board a SeaArk Marine 34-foot Dauntless RAM in the Persian Gulf in 2007. Photo courtesy of the U.S. Navy.

A 34-foot SeaArk Marine Dauntless built for the U.S. Navy's Naval Coastal Warfare Program is loaded onto an Air Force C-5 aircraft for shipment to the Middle East in 2003. Photo courtesy of the U.S. Navy.

cess. Tests were run to certify the engine, speed, sirens, steering, lights, communication, global positioning, and electrical systems.

Domestically, harbor patrol became an important element of homeland security.

In 2003, SeaArk Marine built a 35-foot Dauntless patrol boat for the New York City Police Department Harbor Unit, just one of many boats that SeaArk delivered to federal, state, and municipal agencies across the country to combat the threat of terrorism. Similar boats were built for other agencies such as the City of Boston Police Department, Baltimore Police Department, Kennedy Space Center, and the New Jersey and Virginia State Police.

The people of Monticello don't take patriotism lightly, and they were proud to play a role in the country's security. Ken McFalls, vice president of sales at the time, was quoted in the March 12, 2003 edition of the *Advance Monticellonian* saying, "We make a tremendous contribution to our national defense. The entire SeaArk team takes great pride in being a small part of this massive effort."

In 2002, federal contracts constituted as much as 70 percent of SeaArk Marine's business, a segment that

Russell Peacock and the Pirates

Russell Peacock is currently the quality assurance/ test team manager for SeaArk Marine, following Lester Halbert, who retired after thirty years as a test engineer with the company. Whether or not Russell really understood what his job as a quality assurance manager for a boat company in land-locked Arkansas would entail, only he can say. Whatever the formal job description said, "fending off pirates" must have been in the fine print.

Late in 2004, Russell was charged with the task of delivering a boat to the British Virgin Islands and stopped in the Dominican Republic to take on fuel. There was only Russell, the captain, and a mechanic from SeaArk on board. Suddenly the fellows who were delivering the fuel pulled out guns and said, "What you got on the boat?" Russell answered, "I've got a bag of tools and some lunch meat," hoping that the boat's meager provisions would discourage the erstwhile pirates.

Undaunted, one of them declared that the fuel for the boat would now cost them a lot more than the going rate, in addition to whatever cash Russell and his small crew were carrying. The sale-turned-theft left them with no cash and no groceries.

Now, it must be noted that this was just a short time after the Boston Red Sox clobbered the St. Louis Cardinals in the 2004 World Series. Just as the pirates were leaving the boat, one of them pointed his shotgun menacingly at Russell and said, "I'll have that Boston Red Sox hat, too." Russell gladly handed it over and the pirates went on their way.

These SeaArk Marine workboats were designed for coastal patrol and defense of U.S. naval vessels and facilities. Naval Sea Systems Command (NAVSEA), which purchases vessels for the Navy, in 2002 awarded SeaArk a two-year, $14-million contract for thirty-six security vessels.

SeaArk Marine was presented with a U.S. flag from a SeaArk patrol boat that was deployed in the Northern Arabian Gulf in 2005. The boat provided "anti-terrorist/force protection for maritime assets."

THE DISTRICT ENGINEER AND THE EMPLOYEES
OF
U.S. ARMY CORPS OF ENGINEERS,
GALVESTON DISTRICT
CORDIALLY INVITE YOU TO THE
CHRISTENING
OF
THE MOTOR VESSEL

VANNOY

WEDNESDAY, THE TWENTY-NINTH DAY OF AUGUST
TWO-THOUSAND AND SEVEN
TEN O'CLOCK IN THE MORNING

CORPUS CHRISTI MARINA
LAWRENCE STREET T-HEAD
CORPUS CHRISTI, TEXAS

This Dauntless 35 patrol boat was built for the New York Police Department for harbor patrol following the terrorist attacks of September 11, 2001.

Over the years, the McClendons have received hundreds of invitations like this one to send their boats off in style. This one is for the Vannoy, a hydrographic survey vessel built by SeaArk for the Army Corps of Engineers.

would normally hover around 50 percent. As a result of the added government business, SeaArk Marine added seventy-five employees, bringing the total to around 200 workers.

The challenge SeaArk Marine faced was competing with both defense contracting giants with tremendous resources as well as new start-up companies, both of which could be extremely well connected politically. The new emphasis on national security, and the additional funds being dedicated to it, meant that com-

panies were springing up everywhere to compete with SeaArk Marine. Many of these new entrants to the market disappeared as quickly as they arose, but their presence undercut the more established companies like SeaArk Marine, keeping the entire market in a state of confusion due to price-based selling. Almost invariably, new entrants to the world of military-level construction had no concept of the complexity the product required, and as a result, severely undercut pricing. Despite this incredible competition, SeaArk Marine was able to post

Since the early days of MonArk Boats, Disney has been a major customer for boats used in the entertainment industry. This floating stage built by SeaArk in 1998 is a barge with the operator's area underneath the flat deck. The rig was painted black so that at night the dancers appeared to be floating across the lake.

the highest net income profit in the history of the company at fiscal year end in August 2003. Sales to foreign customers continued to be an important part of that growth with as much as 20 percent of deliveries going outside of the U.S. during this time.

Entertaining and Unusual Boats

Despite the deluge of military contracts, both SeaArk companies had some very unusual and interesting projects during the late 1990s and into the 2000s. Around 1998, SeaArk Boats built electric tour boats, four for use in Arizona and four for use in Virginia. Completely powered by batteries, these boats were for riverwalk areas. Each boat houses twelve batteries and is powered by a Ray electric motor.

It may surprise you to know that Walt Disney Company has the largest non-military fleet in the world. John explained, "Disney has been a big customer of SeaArk Marine as we have built many boats for them including passenger vessels for moving guests, small workboats used for maintenance inside the parks, barges, and several 'floating stages.' Six of these (three

for Florida and three for California) were built for use in the *Fantasia* show, which is performed at night with lights. The floating stage was basically a barge with the operator's area underneath the flat deck. The rig was painted black so that at night the dancers appeared to be floating across the lake."

In 2002, SeaArk Marine built three standard-issue boats for a stunt show based on the Kevin Costner movie *Waterworld* at Universal Studio's water park in Osaka, Japan. A futuristic disaster movie, the boats got special treatment from a California-based company that applied the special finishes to make the boats appear war-torn. As Robin said, "It was very weird to see brand-new boats being beat on, cut on, and smeared with paint to give them the look they needed!"

A New Era of Achievement

In August 2007, SeaArk Marine delivered the largest dollar volume of product in the company's history. As the company marks its fiftieth anniversary, SeaArk Marine alone can boast the production of over 7,500 hulls on waterways around the world.

SeaArk Marine built these boats for Universal Studio's water park in
Osaka, Japan, in 2002 for a show based on the movie Waterworld.

Zach McClendon and two of SeaArk Marine's 40-footers.

Chapter Eight

THE ANSWER TO AN OFT-ASKED QUESTION

Fifty years have passed since Zach McClendon, Sr. called his son at college, beckoning him home to Monticello, Arkansas, to start up a boat business with him and his friend, Norris Judkins. Fifty years have passed since the days that Zach, Jr. spent working with Norris and his son, Elmo, building ten aluminum jon boats at a time and then loading them up on a pick-up truck and hitting the road to sell boats made by an unknown manufacturer to anyone who would buy them.

In that fifty years, Zach McClendon has started up countless businesses, closed the doors on some and sold others, watched his beloved MonArk name pass on to someone else's hands, and resurrected his own recreational boat business, all the while navigating the ups and downs of economic cycles and industry trends. In countless ways, he has played a vital role in shaping and shoring up the community around him and has managed to pass a thriving and financially successful business on to the capable leadership of his own children. It is a true American success story and when you consider the odds against the survival of

independently owned businesses, it is nothing short of a phenomenal accomplishment.

Considering all this, the question that has come up time and time again demands an answer: How does a land-locked aluminum boat builder survive five decades despite heavy competition and a buyout? Situated between pine-covered bluffs in the gently rolling hills of Arkansas and the Mississippi River Delta, the McClendon family's boat-building operation is forty miles from the Mississippi River and 300 miles from the Gulf of Mexico and yet, they have shipped boats to points around the globe. John McClendon recalls a conversation he once had with a Louisiana sheriff to whom he was selling a patrol boat. While they were "sitting and spitting," the sheriff finally asked the question that must have been on his mind through the whole conversation: "Where do you run these boats you make?" John explained with his signature self-assurance that they take all their boats forty-five miles up to the Arkansas River at Pine Bluff to test them. With a mixture of disbelief and amusement, the sheriff said, "Boy, y'all are like a shirt factory in the middle of a nudist colony!"

MODEL PAL612DA

PAL PONTOON BOATS
215 EAST JACKSON
MONTICELLO, AR 71655
PHONE: (870) 367-8502
EMAIL-palpontoonboats@yahoo.com
WEBSITE-www.palpontoonboats.com

*Zach's passion for developing new products and companies is endless as evidenced
by his creation of PAL Pontoon Boats in 2004. This flyer promoted the company.*

Top photo: Robin, Zach, and John pose for a photo for an article in the February/March 2001 issue of Professional
BoatBuilder, *posing the question: How does a land-locked aluminum boat-builder survive four decades?*

Zach McClendon

The answer to the question that's been asked so many times is simple and, according to John McClendon, this family's boat business has survived through "the guts, courage, determination, creativity, and work ethic of Zach McClendon."

While most people think in terms of limitations and are more likely to take the cautious road, Zach McClendon thinks in terms of possibilities. The words "can't" or "too big" are just not part of his vocabulary. He has an enormous tolerance for extreme financial risk and has demonstrated this many times over his career. It is a quality—like many of Zach's traits—that has been both a blessing and a burden over the years.

Zach McClendon is not one of those people who are plagued by self-doubt either. Virtually everyone who has worked with him has come face-to-face with his monumental determination. When he makes up his mind to do something, he does it; the consensus of those around him is solicited, but certainly not required. And while he admits that some of his decisions over the years have been a bit hasty, it's likely because he has a natural ability for assessing a situation, zeroing in on the larger goal, and quickly arriving at a decision.

It's not enough to just say that Zach is a creative person. What is far more accurate is to say that he has a mind that simply never stops working and a natural passion for life that fuels that creativity whether he is thinking about a new boat model or accessory, a community-based landscaping project, or the pile of green bottles in his shed that he plans to turn into a chandelier for his lake house. Thinking creatively is simply the way Zach McClendon walks through the world.

"Zachisms"

Here are some of Zach McClendon's favorite expressions:

"Cash is king."

"We don't know what we don't know."

"There's no such thing as a free lunch."

"You never know—you might learn something."

"Boys, we have barely scratched the surface."

"Great day in the morning!"

"I know. I've been there, Chief."

"If you think about something long enough (bad or good), it will happen."

"Believe me. It will work."

"Don't worry about it—we'll figure out the details later."

"Don't worry about it—we'll make money on the next one."

One that John and Robin hear frequently has one beginning but several possible endings. "Get on an airplane!" could be followed by "Go talk to them about it!" or "Go see how they're doing that!" or "Go see what the hold-up is!" This favorite comment of Zach's attests to the fact that he is never one to hide behind a telephone or shrink from a situation. He prefers an upfront, face-to-face approach whether the issue is money, a potential business deal, or information, and he frequently urges Robin and John to do the same.

The entire Board of Directors of Union Bank and Trust Company, another McClendon family interest, January 2008. Seated left to right: Dave Dickson, Zach McClendon, Jr., and John McClendon. Standing left to right: Ted Carmical, Richard Reinhart, Chuck Dearman, John Porter Price, Frank (Buddy) Carson, Virgil Trotter, Robin McClendon, Dave Wilkins, Wells Moffat, and Charles Jackson.

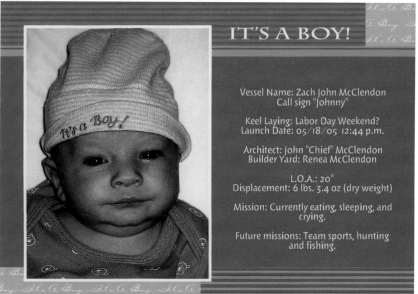

IT'S A BOY!

Vessel Name: Zach John McClendon
Call sign "Johnny"

Keel Laying: Labor Day Weekend?
Launch Date: 05/18/05 12:44 p.m.

Architect: John "Chief" McClendon
Builder Yard: Renea McClendon

L.O.A.: 20"
Displacement: 6 lbs. 3.4 oz (dry weight)

Mission: Currently eating, sleeping, and crying.

Future missions: Team sports, hunting and fishing.

Genius Albert Einstein was said to have a cluttered desk. Zach's is pictured here and Robin admits hers looks just like it.

The third generation of McClendon boat builders, Johnny, arrived on his Aunt Robin's birthday in 2005.

is like a religion. Zach believes that the noblest thing any man or woman can do in this life is work, and work hard. It doesn't matter to Zach if he is building up a boat company, turning around a struggling business, building a deer stand, or planting his garden. He is going to work like there is no tomorrow to get it done."

Zach has passed this work ethic on to his own children and over the years, it has filtered out among MonArk's and SeaArk's employees almost by osmosis. All three McClendons—Zach, Robin, and John—will attest to the dedication of their employees and all three lead, first and foremost, by their own example. At a time when the people in our nation again face economic challenges and growing cynicism, John perfectly expressed

His daughter, Robin, recalls how this habit manifested even when she was a child. "Zach always carried a yellow note pad and a black felt-tip pen that he used to make notes and jot down thoughts. He has switched to a small spiral notebook now, but still has it always ready for his next great thought or design."

All of these qualities would not have gotten Zach McClendon where he is today had it not been for his willingness to put his shoulder to the grindstone to get things done. As his son John said, "Work, for the McClendons, the value of leadership by example when he said, "In a world of endless imposters, Zach is the rare real deal. You can't push a rope; you lead by being out front pulling people forward."

When asked what gave Zach the courage to take on the challenges he's faced, he answered simply, "Faith. I'm optimistic that things are gonna work out. My philosophy is, if you believe something is gonna happen, it's gonna happen. If you *really* believe," he said, tapping his finger to his head, "you can make it happen."

Grooming the Second Generation

Whether or not John and Robin McClendon had intentions of following their father's footsteps into the boat business, they could not have helped but be influenced by both the business itself and their father's solid values. John's earliest memories of the boat plant are of trips he made to the plant with his dad at night. "Zach would need to check on something or look at a boat. He would pick me up on the overhead hoist, or put me up on the forklift," he recalled. "We had a houseboat at the river and a dock where they kept the boats they were testing," John said, referring to Pendleton on the Arkansas River. "For a kid, it was a great thing."

MonArk was a constant presence for Robin and John growing up and now that they are an integral part of the company, "Family life is business life for the McClendons," John said. "Christmas dinner conversations always include boat-building talk, and conversations of the heart begin and end with how a project might be going. Work is viewed as the ultimate elixir of all good health and happiness. There is plenty of recreation; you just sort of have to find it amongst the work."

Being the son and daughter of the boss has not always been easy for them; in fact, just the opposite at times. When John came to work at SeaArk in 1994, he was given a desk in the middle of the sales area, despite the empty office next to it. He asked Zach if he could have that office and received a resounding "No" from his dad. "He didn't want anyone to

Never Judge a Book by Its Cover

In the early days of MonArk, Zach learned a valuable lesson from an old commercial fisherman. He never forgot it, and preaches it to both his children and employees on a regular basis.

MonArk was just starting to gain momentum in the mid-1960s when a crusty old waterman appeared at the door one day inquiring about a semi-custom boat for commercial fishing. Zach had his doubts about the man's financial resources, but wisely kept them to himself.

"He was dressed in near rags and his hands were so rough you could strike a match on them," Zach recalled. "He barely spoke at all and when he did it was kind of a low mumble." The fisherman explained his needs and Zach showed him some boats in the plant and explained how, with some modification, MonArk could produce what he wanted.

After some quick calculations, Zach announced the price. "I just knew I had wasted half the day with this guy," Zach reported, "but he dug down in his coat pocket and produced a wad of cash you could barely get your hand around!" The old man paid the entire price for the boat up front and on the spot.

"Never let something like the way a person looks or talks keep you from taking the time to give someone a chance" is a creed Zach lives by, and it certainly sold more than a few boats over the years.

SeaArk Boats Vice President Steve Henderson (right) with Steve Cooke of Ducky's Marine of Pennsylvania at the factory.

Ken McFalls, vice president of sales for SeaArk Marine, relaxes against a .50-caliber machine gun while extolling the virtues of a SeaArk Marine 40-foot Dauntless patrol boat to a prospective buyer. Ken leads the sales department at SeaArk Marine with unmatched experience, having started in the stock room at MonArk in 1974.

think he had hired his son, put him in a cushy office, and was letting him live the easy life," John explained. "Of all the things Zach has done for me, I think one of the greatest gifts was that he let me sink or swim, make plenty of mistakes, without intervening too much."

Zach admits that he was hard at times on both Robin and John. "Robin had concerns about coming back because then I was a much more overbearing manager," Zach said. Still, as Zach's daughter, Robin occasionally faced the challenges that were unique to her. When she took over the helm of SeaArk Boats, she brought in a consulting firm to evaluate areas for improvement. When it came time for the consultant to present his initial findings, he made the mistake of asking if Zach would be sitting in on the meeting. "After all, you are still daddy's little girl," he said, and that was the end of his consulting work at SeaArk.

With a decade of leadership under their belts, Zach is quick to credit both Robin and John for teaching him the value of a team approach. "They have both done a better job of managing these companies than I ever did," he said. "Part of my problem was I was trying

to manage too many companies. I was spread too thin." However, Zach also recalls hearing his father brag to his peers in the cottonseed oil business about what he and Zach, Jr. were doing in the boat business. With deep respect for each other's contributions and accomplishments, each successive generation of McClendons acknowledges that they could not have done what they did were it not for the generation before.

The People of MonArk and SeaArk

A key asset at MonArk and now SeaArk, and one of the primary contributors to its success, is the people who work there every day, building boats, building the business.

Faithful employees like Ron Echols and Dick Dickinson in the early days recalled Zach's theory: Surround yourself with good people, and give them the authority to handle the job.

MonArk's tradition of loyal employees continues with SeaArk today. "The reason we're successful is our people—we've got a great team," said John, naming just a few who came immediately to mind, such as Lester Halbert and Willie Brennon. Lester, a degreed marine engineer, en-

Zach gives the microphone to Don Law at his retirement party in 2000.

joyed a long career with the McClendon family. Originally hired as engineer at MonArk in the mid-1970s, Lester transferred to become a project engineer at Engineering, Machine & Fabrication (E M & F). He retired as test engineer and quality assurance manager for SeaArk Marine in May 2007. Willie Brennon worked at MonArk and now SeaArk for over thirty years working his way up to his current job as manufacturing manager.

John also gives tremendous credit to Ken McFalls, current vice president of sales at SeaArk Marine. "Of all the salesmen I have worked with, Ken is probably the most realistic one I have met," John remarked. "He is protective of production and engineering and is not the kind of guy who commits us to something unreasonable. That's not his mode. Ken was a Marine in Vietnam, came back after his tour of service, and got his degree in business at the University of Arkansas at Monticello. He went to work in MonArk's supply room and worked his way up." After leaving for another sales position in 1982, Ken returned to SeaArk in 1990.

The loyalty of the MonArk and later SeaArk craftsmen speaks well of both them and the McClendons. Many team members have been with the company twenty-five years or more. Steve Harlow, David Craig, Pat Barnett, Gay Griffith, Don "Smitty" Smith, James Howard, Willie Brennon, Ricky Parker, Dennis Carter, Karen Caldwell, Albert Davis, Ronnie McEntire, Ralph Chastain, Richard Shook, Tony Gober, Richard Stiles, as well as many

others enjoyed long and esteemed careers working for Zach. By notable coincidence, Jim Vance was hired on the exact day John McClendon was born and retired from the company exactly thirty-seven years later to the day.

Robin reflected on another list of longtime team members: "Dick Dickinson just retired at year-end 2008 after many years of service. Dennis Holley has joined us again after being with us in the MonArk days. Several of our team members have been with us from the beginning of the start-up of SeaArk Boats (and before as MonArk), including Jimmy Ray Chancellor, Sammy Reap, David Prince, and Earl Railey. Others that have been with us for years and have been instrumental to the growth of our company are Angela Naron, who has had almost every job in the administrative part of the company and is now our sales coordinator (our dealers LOVE her) along with Randy Weaver, Steve Guin, Robert Gray, Ricky Jordan, Jerry Shepard, Finis Bittle, Trezy Bittle, Jerry Pruitt, and Robert Gordon. We have several members of the Garcia family that have been long and loyal employees. Eduardo, Sr., the father, is a longtime welder with us and his son Eduardo, Jr., is one of our painters. Several other sons work here part-time while they attend college. This was an ongoing arrangement—as his children reach working age, they work here after school and in the summer. They are all very smart and hardworking folks!"

Regarding the skill of SeaArk's workforce, John says, "We're in the middle of pine trees building boats. We have homegrown our own skill, and we've been able to keep a core of highly-skilled workers to ensure that the knowledge base is continued."

Angela Naron toasts Dick Dickinson at his retirement party in 2008.

Having been one of the first companies to manufacture bass boats, the McClendons proudly announce their Stealth Bass Boat for model year 2009.

Standard of Quality = Excellence

In any discussion regarding SeaArk's success, quality has to be front and center.

Admirably, in a world where planned obsolescence is too often used to ensure a company's continued business, SeaArk builds their boats, both recreational and workboats, for the long haul. This emphasis on quality goes back to MonArk's earliest days. Robin observed, "I'll go to shows today and people want to know how Zach is and then tell me a story from years ago. There's a lot of respect and appreciation for Zach and the MonArk name."

Zach was asked to serve on the original voluntary Board of Directors of the Boating Industry Association, which was merged with another organization in 1979 to become the NMMA, or National Marine Manufacturers Association. The NMMA's guidelines for boat-building go above and beyond what the Coast Guard requires for certifying a boat for passengers. Not all of SeaArk Boats's competitors are members. According to Robin, "Following their requirements sometimes means we have to give up other things, for example, extra foam might mean less room for storage boxes. But we've chosen to maintain safety and quality over other features. John and I both try to continue to create the quality products and quality of relationships with our customers that Zach is so well known for—even after all of these years."

Following in his father's footsteps, John served on the NMMA engineering compliance technical committee for several years and had the honor of serving on the board of the American Boat and Yacht Council from 2004 to 2006. The ABYC was formed in 1954 and works with the NMMA and the Coast Guard in setting voluntary safety and construction standards. Membership and participation in these two organizations illustrates the McClendon family's commitment to something much larger than growing their own business—the safety of MonArk's and SeaArk's customers, and the health of the industry as a whole.

Even in the face of an increasingly competitive industry, SeaArk resists the temptation to low-bid competitors, instead maintaining their focus on quality. Said John, "My father's thing was innovation and quality, even to some extent above profitability. He was never afraid to take risks in the name of innovation."

As a result of that focus on innovation and quality engineering and construction, one of SeaArk's most valuable assets is the wealth of intellectual property they hold after fifty continuous years of boat-building experience.

MONARK DEALERS PREPARE TO INVADE MEXICO, SEPTEMBER 7-11, 1977

Many dealers have already qualified for our 1977 trip to The Acapulco Princess, Acapulco, Mexico. Please review the qualifications, rules and regulations. You may be closer to the Border than you realize.

QUALIFICATIONS	Gross Purchase Req'd
1 Person Trip	$38,500
2 Person Trip	$48,500

Note: Trip winners will be able to purchase second trip at pro-rated schedule according to level of achievement. EXAMPLE: $43,500 gross dollars will allow purchase of second trip at 50 per cent of value.

1. Recreational Division orders entered July 15, 1976 through June 17, 1977. All orders must be scheduled for shipment by dealer prior to June 17, 1977.

2. Only invoiced orders paid for by July 4, 1977, will count as qualifying dollars. Credit memos will be deducted from qualifying balance. Account status must be current. In June, MonArk will decide qualification of orders specified for immediate shipment and pending delivery on an individual basis. Freight Charges Do Not Count As Qualifying Dollars.

3. MonArk is final decision-maker in the event of non-specified contingencies.

BEST WISHES,

Don C. Law
Vice President
Corporate Sales

Richard Dickinson
National Sales Manager

In the 1970s and 1980s, MonArk's top dealers were rewarded with trips to fun and exotic locations. The trips were discontinued for many years, but in 2007, SeaArk Boats once again rewarded its top five dealers with a trip to Cabo San Lucas. Pictured in the photo on the facing page are Steve Henderson, Dick Dickinson, longtime representative David Derks, Tami and Sean Finley, and Gloria Dickinson (in hat). The Finleys are with Cook's Boats and Motors in Missouri, one of the company's top dealers.

SeaArk proudly
displays the
NMMA logo
on their
marketing
materials as
a sign of their
strict adherence
to safety and
quality guidelines.

*Zach and lifelong friend John Porter Price prepare to depart on
John Porter's plane for another great houseboating adventure.*

*Facing page: From humble beginnings in the late 1950s,
McClendon boat companies have grown to be major suppliers of
vessels to countries around the world. This map illustrates with
red emphasis that SeaArk boats now span the globe.*

Making a Difference

The well-known news anchor Tom Brokaw once
said, "It's easy to make a buck. It's a lot tougher to
make a difference." There is no doubt as to the enor-
mity of difference Zach McClendon and the MonArk/
SeaArk family have made to their home community of
Monticello, Arkansas.

Their economic contribution alone is noteworthy.
SeaArk Marine itself has a $6-million annual payroll.
When you consider that economists estimate that every
dollar poured into an economy turns at least five times,
that equates to $30 million being inserted into the lo-
cal economy on an annual basis. Adding Drew Foam,
Union Bank, SeaArk Boats, SeaArk Marine, and countless other businesses over the course of the last fifty
years, you begin to see just what kind of impact Zach
has had on the local economy.

An article in the April 27, 2004 *Pine Bluff
Commercial* named Sea Ark Marine as one of the three
largest employers in Drew County. "I am thrilled every day that we employ 206 people," John said. "It's as
important as anything else we do." But beyond simply
employing them, John understands the value of people
believing in what they do. "People want to make a difference," he said. "When you take flat sheets of alu-

minum and turn it into a machine that weighs 61,000
pounds, goes thirty-five miles per hour through the water, and can put out a raging fire 300 feet away, you've
done something."

That kind of pride permeates everything the folks at
SeaArk do, whether it is building boats for oil spill clean-
up, drug interdiction, national security, or boats that provide safe recreation for families across the country, the
people at SeaArk take their work very personally.

Zach and the people of SeaArk have helped the
community in countless ways: rescuing stranded cattle during a flood, assisting with passenger transportation during the flotilla, and rescuing and restoring the
historic Trotter House in Monticello, each time making a difference.

SeaArk is deservedly proud of its record as a corporate citizen. Every year, SeaArk Marine provides
Christmas presents for underprivileged children, gift
boxes to overseas troops, and provides fire safety coloring books, and also supports all the local organizations:
Boy Scouts, Lions Club, Library Fund, Rotary, United
Way, Relay for Life, Safe Prom, Arkansas Sheriff's
Ranches, and many others. An endless stream of school
children, college classes, and community groups are
given tours at SeaArk Marine. In 2002, the Chamber of

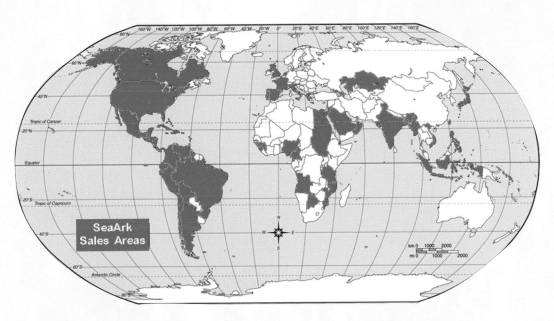

In addition to every U.S. state and territory, SeaArk (formerly MonArk)
has delivered products to the following countries over the course of the last fifty years:

Angola

Antigua

Argentina

Azerbaijan

Bahamas

Bahrain

Bangladesh

Barbados

Batam (Riau Province, Indonesia)

Belize

Bolivia

Botswana

Brazil

British Virgin Islands

Burma

Cameroon

Canada

Cayman Islands

Chile

Christmas Island (Australian Territory)

Colombia

Costa Rica

Cuba

Djibouti

Dominica

Dominican Republic

Ecuador

Egypt

El Salvador

Equatorial Guinea

Former Soviet Republic of Georgia

France

Greece

Grenada

Guatemala

Guinea-Bissau

Guyana

Haiti

Holland

Honduras

Hong Kong

India

Indonesia

Italy

Jamaica

Japan

Jordan

Kazakhstan

Kuwait

Martinique

Mexico

Mozambique

Nicaragua

Nigeria

Oman

Palau

Panama

Peru

Philippines

Portugal

Republic of Guinea

Saipan (Northern Mariana Islands)

Sao Tome

Saudi Arabia

Sierra Leone

Singapore

Slovenia

Solomon Islands

Spain

St. Kitts

St. Lucia

Sudan

Taiwan

Tanzania

Trinidad

Turks & Caicos

United Kingdom

Venezuela

Vietnam

Commerce awarded SeaArk Marine with the honor of being named Drew County's "Industry of the Year."

SeaArk Boats donates to most of the same local charities in addition to Options Women's Shelter, SEARK Concert Association, and the Boys and Girls Club. Robin feels fortunate to have been able to support some causes very close to her heart, often with product donations. SeaArk Boats has donated boats to the Paddlefish Association Research Program, Audubon Arkansas, The Nature Conservancy, Arkansas Game and Fish Foundation, Arkansas Children's Hospital, and the Mississippi River Parkway Commission. For a multitude of reasons, Robin was voted Drew County's "Woman of the Year" in 1999.

Two of SeaArk Boats's charitable projects are particularly significant to Robin: one involved an Indian tribe in Alaska, the other the Susan G. Komen Foundation.

The Athabascan Indian tribe's education area is only accessible by air or water. Here, they bring in teachers to illustrate their way of life, demonstrating basket-making, the use of sweat lodges, cooking, and other wildlife skills. When Robin visited Alaska several years ago, she was honored by being taken to their village via the boat SeaArk donated to see the area and enjoy some moose stew.

In 2008, SeaArk Boats created a camouflage pattern for boats to help support the Susan G. Komen Race for the Cure, an organization devoted to fighting breast cancer. The pink camouflage pattern was painted on six 20-foot SeaArk Boats located in dealerships throughout the country. SeaArk also added a pink ribbon with the company decal symbolizing breast cancer awareness. The proceeds from the sale of each pink boat through December 31, 2008, were donated to the cancer-fighting organization.

SeaArk created a pink camouflage pattern for boats to support the Susan G. Komen Race for the Cure.

SeaArk jon boats, our bread and butter from the beginning...

For fifty years, Zach McClendon has built a dream. He has provided his family and the people of Monticello, Arkansas, with opportunities they might never have had were it not for his courage, determination, and perseverance. He's taken a three-man boat-building operation and overcome buyouts and economic downturns to become two independently successful companies that, despite being land-locked, have provided jobs and a better life for the people of Monticello. He has created the best legacy of all. He has *made a difference.*

Sources:
Professional BoatBuilder, February/March, 2001.
Marine Security Source Book, March/April 2005.

• 1937 •
Zach McClendon, Jr. is born
to Zach, Sr. and Pauline
McClendon in January

• 1956 •
Zach transfers to the
University of Arkansas,
Fayetteville

• 1953 •
Zach, Jr. becomes
an Eagle Scout

• 1955 •
Zach enters
Davidson College in
North Carolina

• 1943 •
McClendon family moves from
Strong to Monticello, Arkansas

• 1958 •
Zach returns
home in May to
start MonArk
with Zach, Sr. and
Norris Judkins

• 1966 •
Camper division of
MonArk is created

• 1963 •
Robin McClendon is
born in May

• 1965 •
MonArk moves to old Root
Manufacturing Plant (current
location of SeaArk Boats)

• 1959 •
MonArk Boat
Company
incorporates
in August

Drew Foam starts up in June

• 1968 •
MonArk purchases
the maritime
division of
Alliance Machine
Company of
Ohio—marks
the beginning of
the aluminum
cathedral hull line

Zach John Scott
McClendon is
born in July

• 1969 •
MonArk fiberglass
boat division starts
in August

Zach partners with
Roberto Chavez
to form Aluminum
Boats of Costa Rica

• 1972 •
Lunker Busters Club and
magazine are started in January

MonArk Custom Craft
established in Jeanerette,
Louisiana, in February

MonArk Shipyards delivers
first towboat, the *MV Christine*

MonArk Shipyards delivers 74-
foot Navy dive support vessel
in March

• 1970 •
MonArk sells
stock to become a
public company

• 1967 •
Zach, Jr. converts an
old government barn
into the Camp at
Mink Track Brake

• 1971 •
Fiberglass plant
destroyed by fire

MonArk Shipyards
in Pine Bluff
established in
December

• 1973 •
Mon Ark Shipyards
(Steelship) and
MonArk Custom Craft
(AlumaShip) are sold
to Joseph Goldstein of
Maryland

Zach, Sr. and Zach, Jr.
purchase the Bank of
West Memphis

• 1975 •

The McFast 7 bass boat is
introduced in January

In February, MonArk builds
the Silver Fox, a custom bass
boat for country music star
Charlie Rich

MonArk builds a 78-foot
Seismograph Catamaran for
Shell Oil in Alaska

• 1979 •

Zach, Sr. and Zach, Jr. sell
Bank of West Memphis

Zach starts up a machine
shop, Engineering,
Manufacturing &
Fabrication (E M & F)

• 1974 •

Bass tournament pros
Jimmy Houston and Bill
Norman sponsored by
MonArk

Bob Lee named president
of MonArk in August

• 1978 •

Zach completes
buy-back of MonArk
public stock

• 1981 •

UniForce Electronics is
started in Little Rock

• 1976 •

Zach, Jr. becomes
president of Union
Bank in Monticello

McClendon Dies Tuesday Night

Zach McClendon Sr., 75, of Monticello, owner and operator of Drew Foam Co. and founder of MonArk Boat Co., died Tuesday night at Drew Memorial Hospital following a lengthy illness.

A native of Strong (Union County), McClendon attended Arkansas College at Batesville, moving to Monticello in 1943 when he bought Drew Cotton Seed Oil Mill, of which he served as president since that time.

He was active in the Oil Seed Producers Association and served as director of the National Oil Producers Association and president of Valley Oil Seed Producers. McClendon founded MonArk Boat Co. in 1959, along with his son, Zach Jr., and N.O. Judkins.

He served on the board of directors at Union Bank and Trust Co. for 34 years (1948-82) and was chairman the past 10 years. He was a member of the board of directors for Citizens Bank

in Strong prior to coming to Drew County and was vice chairman of the Bank of West Memphis from 1972 through 1979.

McClendon was also a director for Ashley, Drew and Northern Railway.

He was a member of First Presbyterian Church, where he served as an elder and deacon.

Survivors include his wife, Pauline Johnson McClendon of Monticello; one son, Zach McClendon Jr. of Monticello; one daughter, Paddy Lee Estes of Washington, D.C.; two brothers, Bob McClendon of McGehee and Harold McClendon of Bastrop, La.; one sister, Blanche Hale of Bastrop, La.; two grandsons and two granddaughters.

Memorial services will be held at 3 p.m. tomorrow (Thursday) at First Presbyterian Church by Dr. Basil Hicks. Burial will be in Oakland Cemetery in Monticello by Stephenson Funeral Home.

The family requests that memorials be made to the building fund of First Presbyterian Church in Monticello.

ZACH MCCLENDON SR.
Dies At Age 75

• 1987 •
UniForce Electronics
is sold to High Voltage
Corporation in
Massachusetts in July

• 1989 •
Sun River Marine
starts up in January

Robin McClendon
joins SeaArk Marine
as marketing director
in July

• 1982 •
Zach McClendon,
Sr. dies in October

• 1985 •
MonArk lands contract
to build 26-foot and 33-
foot boats for the U.S.
Navy in February

Zach John Scott
McClendon becomes
an Eagle Scout in May

• 1986 •
Chuck Mann
becomes president
of MonArk in
September

• 1983 •
Bruce Neimeth is
hired as president of
MonArk in October

• 1988 •
MonArk Boat
Company's
Recreational
Division is sold to
Brunswick in April

Robert Trammel is
named president of
SeaArk Marine

• 1992 •
SeaArk Boats starts
up in August when
Zach's non-compete
agreement with
Brunswick expires

• 1996 •
In June and July, SeaArk employees and
the McClendon family participate in the
weeklong navigation of the Arkansas River to
celebrate the twenty-fifth anniversary of the
McClelland-Kerr Navigational Waterway

Brunswick sells MonArk Boat
Company to Smoker Craft

• 1990 •
Brunswick closes MonArk
boat operations in
Monticello in January

Zach closes down E M & F

SeaArk Boats moves to original MonArk
plant on Patton Street in December

85-foot Passenger Ferry motor yacht is
delivered to ARA Aramark Corporation for
their concession on Lake Powell, Arizona

• 1995 •
July marks the start-
up of International
Waterfront Group

• 1993 •
Due to increasingly difficult
conditions in the industry, Zach
makes dramatic overhead cuts
companywide at SeaArk Marine

SeaArk Marine experiences
highest net income loss in
company history in August

• 1994 •
John McClendon
joins the SeaArk
team in May

Pauline McClendon
dies in September

• 2000 •

Don Law retires as
president of SeaArk
Boats to be replaced by
Charles Clinard in July

After five consecutive
years of losses,
SeaArk Marine posts a
profit in August

The USS *Cole* is bombed
in Yemen in October

Navy contracts start
arriving at SeaArk Marine

On December 7th, an
explosion at SeaArk
Marine results in the
only employee death
caused by accident in
corporate history

• 1998 •

John McClendon
becomes president of
SeaArk Marine in June

SeaArk Marine
completes the Zulu
Project in November

• 2003 •

Supply room at SeaArk
Marine burns in April

Highest net income in
SeaArk Marine company
history is posted in
August at fiscal year-end

• 1997 •

Don Law is named
president of SeaArk
Marine and SeaArk Boats

• 1999 •

SeaArk celebrates
their fortieth
anniversary in
September

Robin McClendon
is promoted to vice
president of marketing
for both SeaArk Boats
and SeaArk Marine in
December

• 2001 •

Robin McClendon is named president
of SeaArk Boats in April

On September 11th, Islamic terrorists
crash hijacked aircraft into the World
Trade Center's twin towers and the
Pentagon. A fourth plane was overtaken
by passengers and crash-landed into
a field in Shanksville, Pennsylvania.
Nearly 3,000 people lost their lives

• 2007 •
SeaArk Marine delivered the largest dollar volume of product in company history in August

Zach, John, Patrick Harris (Zach's nephew), and family friend Anthony Brown take the first and largest legal alligator in Arkansas in September

• 2004 •
Zach starts up PAL Pontoons

• 2006 •
Drew Foam is sold to Pine Creek, LLC in December

• 2008 •
Zach starts up Cloud 9 Pontoon Boats in January

• 2009 •
The SeaArk companies celebrate fifty years in business

• 2005 •
Zach John "Johnny" McClendon is born on his Aunt Robin's birthday in May

ABOUT THE AUTHOR

*P*at Swinger began writing for The Donning Company Publishers after working with them to publish her hometown's history during its sesquicentennial in 2006. Except for the seventeen years she lived in Kirkwood, during which time she received her degree from Washington University in St. Louis, Pat has lived her entire life in O'Fallon, Missouri, and developed an abiding passion for local history. She also enjoys working with organizations and corporations, helping them to tell and preserve their own stories.

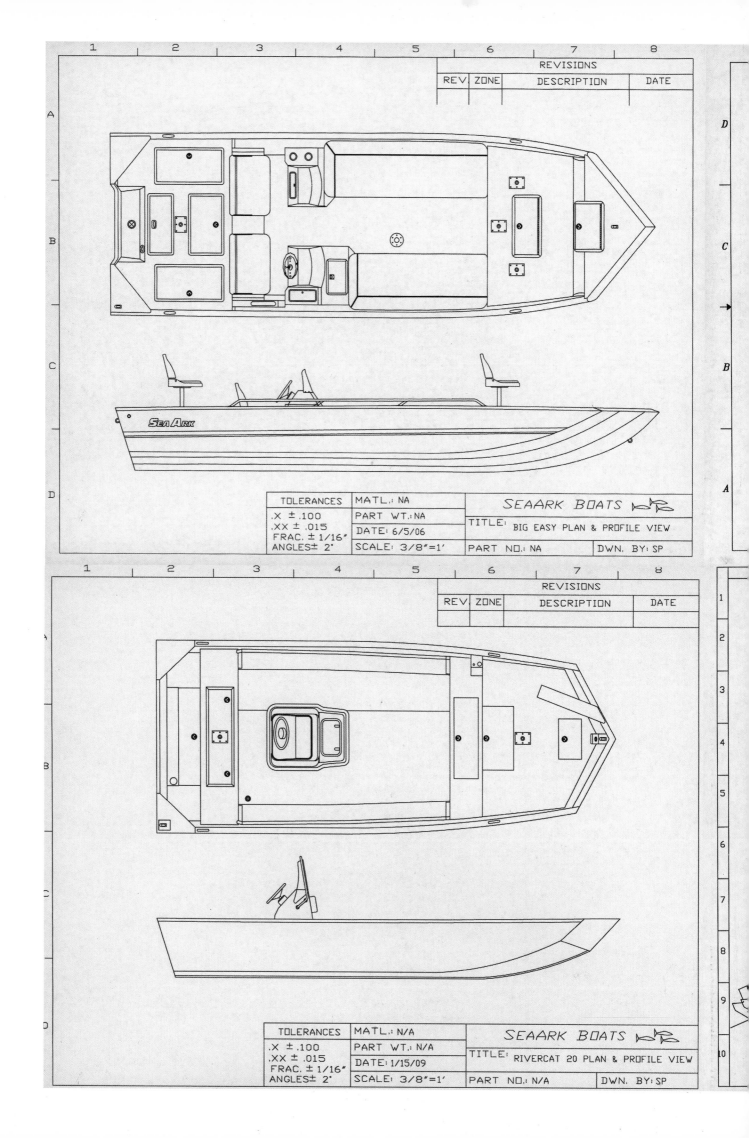

		REVISIONS		
REV	ZONE	DESCRIPTION		DATE

TOLERANCES	MATL.: NA	SEAARK BOATS
.X ± .100	PART WT.: NA	
.XX ± .015	DATE: 6/5/06	TITLE: BIG EASY PLAN & PROFILE VIEW
FRAC. ± 1/16"		
ANGLES± 2°	SCALE: 3/8"=1'	PART NO.: NA DWN. BY: SP

		REVISIONS		
REV	ZONE	DESCRIPTION		DATE

TOLERANCES	MATL.: N/A	SEAARK BOATS
.X ± .100	PART WT.: N/A	
.XX ± .015	DATE: 1/15/09	TITLE: RIVERCAT 20 PLAN & PROFILE VIEW
FRAC. ± 1/16"		
ANGLES± 2°	SCALE: 3/8"=1'	PART NO.: N/A DWN. BY: SP